A MILE FOR THE MILK

Best wishes,

" Alison Hartfield "

(Liba Taylor)

A MILE FOR THE MILK

Alison Hartfield

Illustrated by Judith Wall

BREWIN BOOKS

First published by
Brewin Books Ltd, 56 Alcester Road,
Studley, Warwickshire B80 7LG in 1984
www.brewinbooks.com

Reprinted March 2010

ISBN: 978-1-85858-462-1

A Cataloguing in Publication Record
for this title is available from the British Library.

Typeset in Baskerville
Printed in Great Britain by
Information Press Ltd.

Contents

Acknowledgements

The author would like to thank Punch Publications Ltd., for permission to reproduce the poem by Mrs. F. M. Cornford which originally appeared in "Punch" on April 6th. 1949.

There is an alchemy which in after years transforms most of the weather of our childhood, casting a golden haze of sunshine over a disproportionate part of the time; but, looking back, I know that this particular day needs no such transformation.

I am alone among the gooseberry and currant bushes at the top of our chaotic but satisfying garden. Have I been sent out to pick fruit? It is a usual though not a favourite task. The tinny plop with which gooseberries land in the enamel pie-dish is exhilarating, the grey shaggy lichen on the twigs of the unkempt bushes always fascinates, and the agitated flutterings of disturbed black, white and gold moths has a ritual quality. But the dish is seldom filled without pricks and scratches, and then there is the horrid prospect of "topping and tailing" to follow. Currants are less perilous, and prettier. The red ones hang in jewelled pendant clusters; black ones scent the fingers pungently but pleasantly, and our one stunted bush of white bears so scantily as to give a sense of treasure trove whenever the odd pearly fruit is found. But it is an interminable business. To eat currants straight from the bushes, early on a fine morning when the dew still hangs on them, is really to experience their quintessence; to pick them – no.

The feel of the pie-dish, with its chipped roughened edges and its pleasing innuendoes of pies past and future, is not, however, on my fingers as I write of this vivid day. So am I hiding among the bushes from Phil and Susie? There could be good reason to do so. Phil, two and a half years older than me, and Susie, fifteen months younger, at times enter into an unholy and unfair alliance against me. Lately they have invented a game called "worriting Alison", the joy of which is to disturb me in anything, no matter how innocent, which I happen to be doing, and relentlessly to turf me out of any refuge I imagine myself to have found. The dark little cupboard under the stairs, the horrid mysterious space under my bed (normally tenanted by a Bengal tiger of insatiable ferocity, whose picture in a book has impressed me in terrifying detail), are no secrets to Phil and Susie. Outside, the shed is forbidden ground for playing. The tall rows of raspberry canes afford good cover, but involve a high risk of squashed-raspberry stains on clean clothes meant to last the week. The furthest corner of the garden, where a rank elder hedge screens the rubbish pit, is too obvious as well as too smelly. Shall I be safe among the gooseberry and currant bushes, or will they once again hound me out for pursuit, till with thudding heart and gasping breath, sheer desperation of spirit drives me indoors to violate our unspoken code and tell the Grown-Ups?

Again, the overtone of recollected persecution is absent. Today I have achieved, whether deliberately or accidentally, a short space of solitude, which is a rare enough condition in our small home. And I am caught up in a new experience, the realization of myself. Why am I Alison, and not Phil or Susie? What has made me the being that I am? How strange that I should suddenly be aware of the me-ness of me! Yet I have always been here, and not to have existed would be inconceivable, as is the idea of ever ceasing to exist. Briefly I consider this mystery, which even then seems to me to hold the seeds of my immortality. It is one of those suspended moments of wonder, of which the Grown-Up world would hardly suspect a skinny six or seven year old. Round glasses and deplorably straight mousy hair; an endless capacity for "showing-off" (why do they call it that, when I am just being natural?), for saying the wrong thing at the wrong time, and for dropping such things as enamel pie-dishes resoundingly on stone floors – that's me, as far as they know.

The moment passes. I return to normal life – a ceaseless, scrabbling, mostly joyous activity throughout days never long enough. But the wonder is to recur. Later, I am to extend it to the beings of other people; to see Phil, Susie, the children in my mother's village school, as other separate, secret personalities, showing, as I do, only small facets of their real selves to the world. Later still, away from the quietness of this village which was my childhood universe, I am to step back from the press of a London rush hour crowd, suddenly realizing how its striving anonymity masks an unimaginable complexity of purposes, hopes, fears, tragedies and ecstasies. As I stand among the young children I teach, I am to draw back in awe, catching my breath at the sudden vision of each one's depth of precious uniqueness, and of my own unworthiness to play a part in nurturing it. Last of all, perhaps, I am to see my parents as disparate personalities in their own right, rather than as the extensions of us their children that they have long seemed to be; and I am to marvel again and again at the rich diversity of interlocking individualities which forms the pattern of family life and of human relationships.

From marvelling to writing has been a slow, gentle and inevitable progress. Our shared childhood in the stone-built school house had its own uniqueness, while partaking of the flavour of country childhoods everywhere. Looking back, it has seemed to me a goodly heritage and one worth offering to others. Perhaps, too, as we grow further away in time from the children we once were, we feel the need to revive them, to celebrate our happy and carefree seasons, and to re-affirm an inner continuity with our earliest selves. Over fifty years on, that skinny child among the gooseberry bushes is still, miraculously, me. I have never ceased to wonder, and as I wonder, I remember.....................

Tucked under the edge of the North Wiltshire Downs lay our village, a cluster of shabby cottages around the lovely, ancient little church, flanked by Vicarage and Manor House, Home Farm, school and pub. A straggle of Council Houses and a network of lanes linking up the outlying farms and their tied cottages, and, a mile or so away, the lower village with a Post-Office-cum-shop and another pub – just this, for years, marked the boundaries of our childhood world. Unspoilt and even primitive when we lived there, the village has survived a period of decay during which it became a sadness to re-visit it. Now it has been "discovered". The once shabby cottages are smart with gleaming new thatch, carefully blacked timbers and the standard issue of carriage lamps. But a well-intentioned conservation order, by restricting building, is slowly killing the village. The school is already dead. Little houses which lack romantic "suitability for conversion" are empty and beginning to crumble. Young people are moving out, leaving the elderly to lament the old days in solitude. Seeing the village now, you might find it hard to believe that it was the backdrop to a childhood of unimaginable richness.

But if you are old enough to leave the intimate setting of our garden, where every stone is a familiar, every change in ground level as natural to your legs as is the turn halfway up the dark creaking staircase inside the house – if you can venture beyond the school playground, which outside school hours is an accepted extension of our territory, then the riches are there for your possession. Take the field path from the top of the garden, dive with it through a dark little larch copse, dodge round a flat upright stone supposed to prevent horse-drawn vehicles from attempting the footpath, and you are on the gravelly road up the Hill, climbing transversely across a wooded slope called the Hangings. Echoing to the harsh bark of foxes and the melancholy hooting of owls in the winter; a tapestry of gold, flame and russet in autumn; a miracle, every spring, of tender brown twig and pastel-green new leaf, in summer it is alive with cuckoos, shouting incessantly to each other and eventually causing my mother to "drat that bird". (Oh that we now had cuckoos in drattable numbers.) Climb the Hill, anyway, your short legs aching, for the gradient is steep. Pass the disused chalk quarry where, if you are in the mood, fossils may be found – shells and ammonites and even, once, what looked like a petrified sea-urchin, which Phil treasures to this day. Arrive panting at the top, where the banks are grassy and great blue and white violets flower in

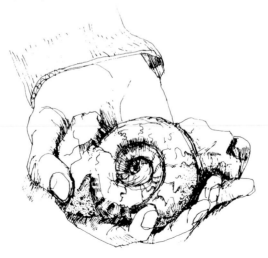

season. Walk just a quarter of a mile further to find the Cherry Copse, a froth of white blossom, and then take your choice – the green track to the nearest village, and back across the lower fields, through our churchyard and so home? The turning to another village, straggling, untidy, inducing a pleasant sense of the superiority of our village, and leading past some old sweet chestnut trees whose low horizontal boughs are perfect for swinging? Or shall we take another fork, along another leafy lane, to yet another village which we have to acknowledge is actually tidier, better groomed than ours? In the distance we can see the lovely bare sweep of the Downs, the pale skyline broken here and there by elegant clumps of beech trees. To reach their heights and visit the wonders of ancient barrows and hill forts which they hold in their drowsy, silent keeping needs a whole day's expedition with provisions, so not today. A little nearer we spy the White Horse, staring chalkily out of the downland turf from which it was cut, who knows how many years ago. Satisfied that our landmarks are all in place, we turn in our chosen direction. And now you must know that we can tell you exactly where to find the earliest celandine, the pale broom-rape skulking unhealthily beneath the dark trees, the improbable but beautiful bee-orchis, the meadow saxifrage, primroses thick as butter, cowslips, bluebells and early purple orchids by the hundred, and the one white-flowering plant (my father's discovery) of the heavenly blue meadow cranes-bill, the flower of all flowers in our country kingdom. For this is lore that we have absorbed since we were pushed out in the "sulky" (pushchair to you), or staggered beside it – and it is all ours, breath of our being, "splendour in the grass and glory in the flower". As we turn homewards at last, eyes bright, hot or cold hands filled with flowers or sprays of berries as the season wills (but what you pick you must carry home and put in water with care), remember that you have only touched the fringes of our world. Elsewhere are mysterious little ponds with strange rushes and water-weeds; other woods and copses with their individual treasures; pastures full of mushrooms or blackberries; little hidden lanes where the rainwater lies like milk in the chalky ruts. You may note the growth of young green corn to heavy gold, wisely predict an early haycutting from the look of the thick rippling meadow grass, delight in the young farm creatures, each kind born at its appointed time; for such is the wealth of our small, gloriously inefficient mixed farms and holdings. Only shut the gate behind you, and keep to the paths around the growing crops, as we all do in the country, and you may go as you will, garnering riches to last you all your life through.

So what did it matter if our world was long bounded by the distance which we could walk? Here walking was the natural, almost the only way of life. My mother's aged bicycle was the only one in the family. The number of cars in the village, when we were small, could almost have been told on the fingers of one hand. We used to rush to our gate to see them go by, with shouts of "Motor!" Only later came a bus service two or three times a week, plying the twenty miles between two towns and weaving a leisurely course among the villages scattered along the way. So roundabout was the route that you could miss the bus in our village and catch it in the next by sprinting smartly over the timeworn path across the fields; but this was not often necessary, as in true country-bus tradition the driver would wait for latecomers, carry parcels from village to village, and take messages between households a few miles apart. I joy in the memory of the leisurely pace of life in my childhood, and in my deep country roots. I am grateful that I can remember grey dawns when we jolted the five miles to the nearest station in a farmer's horse-drawn trap, to catch an excursion train for a rare, ecstatic day at the seaside. I have watched great patient horses plod endlessly over the land drawing plough or harrow, have seen their unhurried journeys

between field and farmyard with fragrant loads of honest manure and delicate hay, and have myself ridden bumpily and enjoyably in empty hay wagons. And the clear metallic ring of hammer on anvil from the forge just up the Hill was as familiar a childhood sound as the ticking of our own clock.

I won't deny that our isolation did have some drawbacks. No doubt the village was much inter-married. And everybody, of course, knew everybody else's business – though we were long shielded from the darker and more unkind aspects of village gossip. We missed out on many experiences which today's children take for granted, and our outlook was, I suppose, parochial in the extreme. But there is much, so much to be said for knowing a small community, a small area, in real depth – Jane Austen's "piece of ivory two inches square". People had to develop their own resources and amusements, and most of these were harmless enough, though there was a fair amount of Saturday night drunkenness, and summer evenings tended to herald hasty marriages. There was little, if any, of the juvenile delinquency so often ascribed to boredom. But it is the lack of inner rather than of material resources which bores. We, at least, were very rarely bored, in spite of the almost complete lack of "laid-on" entertainment. Radio was in its early days – I believe that ours, occupying a whole table with goodness knows what paraphernalia of receiver and loudspeaker, dry batteries and "wet" accumulator (collected for re-charging once a week), was the first in the village. The Brownie Pack and Guide Company, inspired and largely organized by my mother, when they came, were a boon. A small branch of the Women's Institute met regularly, their headquarters an Army hut acquired for the purpose and standing to this day, though last time I saw it, it looked as if it would not hold together much longer. It seemed a most desirable place when we penetrated it for rare village events – a missionary exhibition, lantern slides of Oberammergau, the Brownie and Guide party. Nobody worried that it was without sanitation, till wartime evacuees over-crowded the school and the Hut was commandeered as a classroom, and hastily equipped with toilets. The school was the only other meeting place, but except for elections and Parish Council meetings, it was little used.

The church (and to a lesser extent the chapel) was a focal point of everyone's life. Sunday School and choir, in their heyday, gave shape and purpose to children's Sundays. Whole families came to church with clockwork regularity, in all weathers, though there were of course those who came only for christenings, weddings and funerals. It was central to our lives from an early age, though we were never made to go to church. It was an outing, a privilege, a foot over the edge into the Grown-Up world. I was never bored in church, nor, I believe, did I disturb other people. In summer I loved to see the sunlight strike through the East window, dappling its vivid blues and scarlets on to the stone chancel step. On winter evenings, warm and lamplit, the little church seemed a haven of tranquillity after a blustery, wet, or cold walk down to it in the dark. The sonorous words of Bible and sermon rolled pleasurably over my head, kindling sparks of barely grasped meaning here and there at first, moving slowly towards understanding later. The smallest of us could cuddle up to my mother during sermon time, so that a loving human closeness mingled with a sense of other-worldliness, gradually giving us all a foundation of belief which, thank God, we have never lost. Hymns we loved – we were early readers and sang lustily through them, more or less in tune. Psalms began to register somewhat later, and again, I am thankful that this early enjoyment has imprinted both hymns and psalms so well upon my memory that they are there to fall back on, any time of day or night. In our navy blue reefer coats and red-and-navy velvet tam-o'-shanters (you wore a hat of some kind for church even at the age of four), our solid little legs encased in the good grey socks knitted by my mother and disappearing into stout black shoes or boots, there we stood, enjoying every minute, in the knowledge that the church was ours. We felt a personal pride in the beautiful Jacobean pulpit, the elaborate alabaster monument to a local philanthropist, the bells that seemed always to be manned for ringing. As we grew older this pride was enhanced by our attendance (and later, teaching) at Sunday School, and the birth of a choir – a real surpliced choir – of which we became members when my mother took over the playing of the organ. Precious, if hectic, Sundays thereafter – morning services when my hands clasped in prayer still carried the smell of carrots or parsnips prepared ready for cooking as soon as we got home! when Sunday dinner was followed rapidly by Sunday School, and Sunday tea by Evensong. Even more precious festivals! the culmination of weeks of practising carols or simple anthems, to be rendered by us the choir, our clean surplices a-crackle with starch. The anxiety as to the decorations – would there be berried holly enough for Christmas, primroses for Easter? For Harvest Festival there was never any lack of produce. "All is safely gathered in" joyfully sang the whole village (or so it seemed), and sideways glances would be cast by proud farmers, gardeners and tillers of allotments, to where their own sheaf of corn, basket of apples or mammoth marrow stood praising God with them. Then there was the Feast – the summer Sunday when, by tradition, the entire congregation of the little daughter church in the village across the fields trooped over to worship with us in the evening, cramming the church with best suits and emotion, building expectantly up to the last hymn, which had to be "Onward, Christian Soldiers". How we all sang! The choir and organist tried to keep a semblance of pace going, but failed completely as the congregation, relishing every note, bawled (there is no other word for it) louder and slower at every verse, till the last note died away and the Feast was over for another year. Or not quite over, for on Feast Day the Vicarage and sometimes the Manor gardens were opened for all to enjoy. The Vicarage garden in June was breathtaking, a paradise of grassy paths among cleverly landscaped beds of flowers, shrubs and trees, some rare and exotic, all beautiful. At the Manor great sweeps of open lawn led down to a pond (but we called it the lake) with real waxy-white, gold-centred, pink-blushed water-lilies. It was a green coolness, a different but wholly memorable experience. The two villages walked round, admired, chatted, exchanged news accumulated since this time last year. Old pupils greeted my mother, some with a newly found confidence, for were they not now equals in the world of work? Others were red-faced and gauche, as though "Governess" (her usual title, as in other village schools of the period) would still be marking their smudgy exercise books tomorrow. As the warm summer dusk fell, the strollers thinned out, and the children running round the grassy paths were rounded up and taken home to bed. The church had brought us all together. It mattered, signified still as it should. Content, we too were gathered for home and bed. And to this day, "Onward, Christian Soldiers" can still bring a tightness to my throat and prick my eyes with tears.

But back from Sundays to everyday life. Primitive, as I have said, the village was in many ways. Needless to say, we had no electricity, gas, or modern sanitation. Everyone took candles and oil lamps for granted; likewise the odorous little house "up the garden" which concealed the earth closet. More classily, there might be a chemical closet in outhouse or shed. Flush toilets graced, as far as I know, the Vicarage and Manor only. But parts of the village did have piped water – unusual for the time and the area. The school and our adjoining school house were the last on the system, hence the first to feel any stress such as a burst pipe elsewhere, or even a cottager filling her copper for a Monday boil and wash. After a time we achieved a galvanized tank in the scullery, so that we always had a reserve from which to pump. If all else failed, there was a clear spring a couple of minutes' walk away, and as my father loved to drink its ice-cold water, we made many a little pilgrimage to fetch it for him. There must have been some kind of drainage system too, for I know that water emptied down our sink disappeared into the bowels of the earth, but how and where it went, I have no idea.

In the lower village, the little shop carried a stock of basics, and I dimly remember that Old Shep's wife, our next door neighbour, at one time ran a minute rival establishment in her front room. But most of our supplies came from farther afield. A travelling ironmonger's van delivered paraffin, our mainstay for cooking and heating as well as light. Fruit and fish could be bought once a week – Tuesday, I think it was. The "Co-op" butcher called on Fridays, a gentle, rather sad man. "Butch-ay" he would call in melancholy tones, a great contrast to the ebullient *"How*-d'you-do" of the ironmonger. "Got a nice bit of steak for the master's supper" he told my mother one Friday, "sweet as a lily it is". And when the firm replaced his battered old van by a glossy new one, he insisted on Phil's viewing it – why, we never quite knew. "Your big girl did ought to see my new van. She'd appreciate it." So Phil duly trotted down to the gate, and appreciated, and "Butch-ay" went on his way, for once a shade less melancholy.

We patronized, I think, a succession of travelling grocers. The Co-op, the World's Stores, the International – did they all visit the village during the same period, or did they succeed each other? At all events, groceries were delivered. Some of the firms sent a polite little man round to collect your order, which was then delivered (more or less) on the appointed day. The Co-op era was a handy one, for the grocery delivery man would take shoes to the firm's repair department and return them, mended, the following week. I was always hard on shoes and mine made many such trips. ("Alison's shoes need heeling AGAIN"). Bread came from closer at hand, two or three times a week – golden crusty loaves, still hot to the touch. Take a cottage loaf (if your mother will let you), tear the two halves apart, revealing a soft hollow on the top of one half and a corresponding gentle dome on the underside of the other. Slice this off, steaming, butter it and eat… We used to beg and even fight for "the cushion" as we called it. An occasional treat was a real Wiltshire lardy cake, loaded with currants and sultanas, shining and sticky with sweetness on top. And I remember for years paying threepence-halfpenny for a large loaf.

Vegetables can have had little sale in the village, for everyone had a garden, or an allotment, or both. Until my teens I can't recall that we ever bought any vegetables but potatoes. With traditional country open-handedness, good yields would be shared around the village. "Dad's carrots 've come on a treat this year, so he thought you'd like a few". We reciprocated when we could, mostly with soft fruit, for in a good season we had raspberries and gooseberries enough and to spare. Eggs, Christmas poultry, and rabbits (a great standby) came from one or other of the farms. Before the

Second World War, eightpence or ninepence was the average price, and if the farmer asked tenpence you expected a really outsize bunny. And then there was The Milk………

I vaguely recall a period when our milk was brought to the door, but this soon came to an end, and a daily ritual of "going for the milk" began. There must have been plenty of older pupils at the school who would have picked it up on their way for a nominal fee, so I imagine that my father's dislike of "being under an obligation", and perhaps some awkward breakdown in the original arrangement, accounted for the decision that we should fetch it ourselves, and for many years we did. At first my father went with us. But soon, after a serious illness, he had to adopt a pattern of late rising, and the task became Phil's, with Susie or myself accompanying her on alternate days during the week, and the three of us going at weekends. (There was a time when Phil received the vast sum of sixpence a week in return, but this lapsed very quickly – pocket money in our family was always an uncertain affair). Looking back down the vista of the years during which our small figures plodded day after day, regardless of the weather, the mile down the lane to the farm and the mile back, picking up our two quarts of milk in one tin milk can and leaving another ready for the next day, I have come to see "going for the milk" not merely as epitomizing our whole way of life, but as a central experience, one of the most informative, even educational, influences I have ever had. If this seems improbable or incomprehensible, I hope to convince you of it later.

Shopping for clothes was done mainly by post. The arrival of Williams' or Oxendale's new catalogue was a yearly thrill, heralding hours of scanning the well illustrated pages for wonders we knew to be out of reach, as for years my mother knitted everything that could be knitted, sewed everything that could be sewed. But there were occasional orders from the magic pages – as well as the asset of last year's catalogues turned over to us for cutting out. One firm, I recall, in its section of babies' layettes, promised a second one, FREE, "if you have already ordered one of our layettes and it turns out to be twins". We thought this was unparalleled generosity, and took a lot of convincing that the firm would not lose on the deal. My mother made once-a-month trips on her bicycle to the nearest small town five miles away, to stock up on a strictly limited range of necessities like toothpaste, Owbridge's Lung Tonic for our winter colds, and the delicious "Roboleine", or loathsome cod liver oil, supposed to fortify us against the next winter. Before Christmas she would make an expedition of really epic proportions to the larger and more distant town of Swindon to buy our presents. How she did it (as with so many of her achievements) I shall never know. She would pedal off cheerfully in the morning, returning often after dark, tired but triumphant, exhilarated by this rare contact with the outside world, her bicycle loaded, dangling, with an amazing array of bags and parcels. Try riding twelve miles in the dark with, among other things, three scooters attached to your bicycle – she did it once! This was the normal, the only way to shop. Later, when the Bus started to run, new worlds opened up. We might not use it more than two or three times a year, but the prospect and then the recollection of "going to Swindon on the Bus", with perhaps two shillings (real bounty) to spend at Woolworths', was something we could live on for weeks…

So, we managed to eat (economically), to be clothed (economically), to take our near-isolation for granted, and for years to find our village life absorbing. There is no lack of drama in a small rural community. Indeed the sense of drama in everyday things is a heightened one. World affairs are remote, perhaps dangerously so – the real events are the births, deaths, and marriages, the rare movements of farm workers in an area where the departure of one family can seriously reduce a school roll. Even more rare, the retirement of a farmer with the consequent sale and re-occupation of the farm, or the real trauma (once in our lifetime in the village) of a change of Vicar. For years my mother ran her school with the same two assistants, and again, changes here, when they came, seemed to shake the very foundations. Occasional tragedies stunned the entire community – a much wanted baby stillborn; the wiping out of farm stock by foot-and-mouth disease; death or injury by farm accident – all these we knew, and in some way shared. Old people withered and died, cancer being all too frequent, and it was common then for a collection to be taken round the village, not for flowers but to help the bereaved with funeral expenses.

Old people should have pride of place in any village portrait gallery. Prematurely bent by years of damp housing, weatherworn and rosy from their outdoor lives, slow and burring of speech, they fascinated us, but held an element of fear when encountered "on the way for the milk". This was partly due to our natural shyness; but also, I think, as we had been told to be polite and pass the time of day, we were embarrassed at being unable to follow what they were saying. Our neighbour, Old Shep, retired after goodness knows how many years devoted to his (or his master's) sheep, lame but indomitable, loved to waylay us for a chat. I can hear the rise and fall of his old voice now, feel myself straining to catch a few words to which to respond. His "bard laig" recurred frequently; and he blamed the weather on "they flyers" – the aeroplanes which, with increasing temerity, began to trouble our peaceful skies. Honest and God-fearing, regularly as clockwork on weekdays he dragged himself down past the school to feed his handful of chickens, and to work his allotment just below the school playground. On Sundays, dressed in his best black suit, with equal regularity he dragged himself to church visiting the allotment on the way back – for inspection only – he would not have lifted a finger to touch it on a Sunday. Dear Old Shep – I salute you and your kind, a vanished breed. Vanished, too, are the likes of old Mrs. Binns, whom I can just remember leaning over her cottage gate at a great age, wearing a starched and goffered snowy white sunbonnet. (Just such a sunbonnet, believe it or not, I saw lovingly handled and displayed, as an antique of some value, on a television programme only the other day). Down in the lower village, a group of gypsies had made their base, under the matriarchal rule of Grandma – Smith, we will call her, though it does little justice to her colourful personality. I don't know that I ever saw her, but her legendary reputation was enough. I believe that she ruled her menfolk with a rod of iron, though she must have been generous with the beer money on Saturday nights, judging by the men's melodious progress home after closing time. She was certainly instrumental, and adept too, in keeping the grandchildren from attending school for some years – the eldest managed to evade it completely. The women wore ear-rings and brooches made from gold half-sovereigns, so their pickings from paper flowers, clothes pegs and so forth must have been good. In another league altogether was the ageing widow of the Manor House, living out her last years there with a sad and gentle lady companion. Veiled, and dressed in black, they were sometimes to be seen around the village; indeed I can remember their paying a state call at the School House at least once. They filled us with awe, and we found it very difficult to manage to greet them as polite children should.

As I look back, my mind floods with personalities, each one standing out sharp and clear against the village setting, each having an accepted niche and role there. Oddities were accepted in our community – the grown woman "not quite like other people" who had happily continued to attend the school till she was twenty, the strange, wild-eyed boys of one family who learned little at school but were the valued performers of small tasks, filling the kettles and stoking the "Tortoise" stoves. Today you rarely see children with rickets, but we knew a whole family who stumbled their way through life as a result of this condition, "book-learning" again making little impression on them. Attempts were made to send them to a special school, but their mother would not hear of it. "My children are all right – just a bit old-fashioned". Large families threaded their way through the school – five, six, eight or even ten of them in succession, some slow and contented, some bright and aspiring. Each new child to enter was already a familiar name and face, long before the first day at school. Petted for a few days by the older girls, they were quickly absorbed into the school community. We watched them from a little distance, saw their personalities unfold in the playground, listened with rapt attention to all that my mother told us of their progress, their entertaining or mildly outrageous deeds. We knew all the parents by name, and most by sight; were aware of the fathers' occupations and the subtle gradations in village status which distinguished farm labourers, grooms, the roadman, the Vicarage and Manor gardeners, the post-master, sexton, smallholders and the occasional railway or United Dairies worker; these just about covered the range of employment available. Boys tended to follow their fathers on to the land; indeed many of them were already working there, outside school hours, as soon as they were old enough and strong enough to be of any use. For girls, there was little beyond "good service" at the Vicarage, the Manor, or one of the more prosperous farms, with perhaps an occasional opening for the really ambitious in the shops of the nearest small town. Early marriage claimed and absorbed most of them, and it was only the war and post-war years, bringing transport within everyone's reach, which widened the opportunities – and, by draining the village of its young people, began to sound its death-knell.

But that was still to come. Unconscious that we belonged to a vanishing way of life, we lived it to the full, savouring each member of the small galaxy of personalities in which, for good or ill, every individual stood out, counted, from youngest to oldest, from village scamp to upright churchwarden, from gipsy to Vicar. Can you wonder that I think of my village childhood in terms of riches?

In and Out of School

The village school has been immortalised for many of us by the gentle and perceptive pen of "Miss Read". To town dwellers her books must have come as a revelation of a world largely unknown, but to country people they are a mirror, faithful and nostalgic, of the kind of education and ethos which we took for granted. My mother, past retirement age when the books began to appear, rejoiced in each successive one, but her appreciation was tinged with a little sadness, for she had often said that she not only could, but one day would, write a book about her village school; now she felt that "Miss Read" had pre-empted her and that there was no place left for her book. We did our best to persuade her to go ahead, and I think it is a real loss to the reading public that we failed, for she was an able writer; and her story, set in a world some twenty-five years earlier than that of "Village School", would have complemented it with a charm and quality of its own. I cannot capture the flavour as she would have done, from her unique position as "Governess" and centre of this little world. For nearly twenty years she ruled it, firmly but never harshly, a pillar of strength to the whole village as well to us her family, who stood a little outside the school microcosm, yet to whom it was so natural a habitat that we entered, left and re-entered it often and effortlessly throughout our years in the village.

For "school" was as inescapable and inevitable as the air one breathed – always there, mingling with home, as close as party walls could make it. A bricked-up archway in the wall between the Big Schoolroom and our hallowed Front Room showed that they had once led off each other. I do not know whether the school itself, a stone building (with Gothic aspirations, and a little bell-tower from which the school bell was rung twice a day), and the house which was home to us, had been built as one unit, though in my recollection they appear to have been contemporary. Perhaps the archway was bricked up when the Infant Room was added to the original school building, and a lean-to scullery and shed to the "two up, two down" house. All that was before our time, but I do have vague memories of the building of an additional "lobby" for the children's coats, and new "offices" for the boys in a suitably secluded corner of the playground. A dank passageway at the back of the school led to the girls' "offices" – a sociable set up of the family three-holer type with long wooden seats over sturdy buckets. They were kept well emptied and disinfected, and it was not till the wartime evacuees found them distasteful that we began to wonder ourselves...

"Tortoise" stoves (who else remembers them?) heated both the Infant Room and the Big Room; they were lit every morning by the cleaner of the moment (we enjoyed, or endured, a succession of Mrs. Pringle-like characters)*, and stoked during the day by the older boys. Every year a supply of wood faggots – bundles of hazel, willow and ash, rather like pea-sticks, secured around with withies – would arrive, to be stacked neatly in a corner the playground for the next winter's kindling. Climbing, nay, mountaineering on the faggots was a pastime of ours which was unpopular with the Grown-Ups, though not quite forbidden. It was hard on shoes, and easily productive of rips in coats and socks. But we loved it

– the astringent smell of the wood, the chance of finding a ladybird, or an odd twig still bearing tiny hazel-catkins or pussy-willow, the thrilling creakings of the pile as we clambered about, the sense of exploration and height (when you are small, even four feet extra gives you an entirely different view of life) – and climbed with just enough caution to avoid a complete ban on the pursuit. Somewhere, too, there was a vast coke-heap from which buckets were filled for the stoking of the stoves, but I don't recall that this had any sporting possibilities.

The interior of the school was predictable – a dull and sensible decor of chocolate and cream which my mother revolutionized into daffodil yellow and green as soon as she had the chance; heavy iron-bound desks for two, and even some long desks for six-in-a-row, tops lifting to give access to storage lockers, inkwells set into the right-hand corners. By degrees my mother was able to replace some of them by chairs and tables. The long desk seats were relegated to the edges of the playground, where their solid oak and cruel cast-iron (try cracking your ankle-bone on it!) withstood the weather almost indefinitely, and endless games could be played along, over, under, and round them. The Infants, I think, got their little chairs and tables first. They were a slightly privileged race, with a dolls' house in a corner of the room and a faint admixture of play in their work, though work was what the school was for – there was never any doubt as to that. A few pictures clung to the walls, and I can see even now the one that impressed me the most, cut from a newspaper and captioned "Our little Princess Elizabeth, now just two years old". I am not much older than Her Gracious Majesty, so this is clearly an early recollection from my somewhat transitory experience in the Infant Room.

The Big Room held two classes, a moveable screen separating the "Juniors", eight to eleven years old or so, from my mother's own class of "Seniors" up to fourteen. Photographs show bonny, ripe-looking older girls side by side with huge brawny boys, many of them still wearing, and almost bursting out of, "short trousers" of an amazing length to our eyes of today. As time went on, my mother knew all their families and their antecedents inside out, backwards and upside down, and reached the stage of admitting five-year-olds whose parents she had taught. Skirts shortened and trousers lengthened. But in our early years nothing seemed to change. The Big Room children effortlessly, it seemed, listened to the right teacher at the right time. Singing was taken all together, and must have widened the children's horizons considerably, for not only did they learn traditional airs, "Bluebells of Scotland" and such like, but there were also excursions into higher things. An inspector, nearing the school and pausing to read his map, was astonished to hear the strains of "Die schöne Müllerin" from the man behind the plough in the next field. It had been his favourite song at school.

My mother had a fine scorn for so-called "modern methods" (which led to many an educational argument in later years, when one after another we began to follow in her teaching footsteps). The Infants learned to write a copper-plate type of longhand from the start – no messing about with a simplified script. She believed in the value of learning by heart, so that we lived with the rhythmic chanting of tables, slow at first, then gradually accelerating and gaining in pitch and emphasis. "Nine sixes are fifty-four, ten sixes are *sixty*," the class would drone, then on into the glorious crescendo and thump of the final "*Eleven* sixes are *sixty*-six, *Twelve* sixes are seventy-*two*", on a note of relief and triumph. The Art work of the older boys was a thing of beauty to our admiring eyes, though today it would rate only a shake of the head, at best, in educational circles. They meticulously copied pictures of flowers, birds or animals, shading them in with their paint-box colours, while the girls worked on needlework or knitting. The finished products were proudly displayed on wall or cupboard. Once, and once only, was my mother summoned from her hurried midday meal back in the house with us, during which she was supposed not to be disturbed for anything less than the arrival of an Inspector. A wild older boy (today he would be deemed "maladjusted") had, in a fit of dare-devilry, slung the dregs of his dinner-time cocoa over the sacred art exhibition. Nemesis, in the form of "Governess's" seldom used cane, was swift, but the foundations had been shaken and took a little time to settle again.........

In spite of her avowed dislike of new-fangled methods, my mother clocked up several "firsts" in the County – first school to start using the B.B.C. broadcasts for schools, first to take up poultry-keeping and later (I think) first to experiment with the breeding of rabbits. I remember the "Seniors" crowding into our living-room for those early "wireless lessons", sitting on the floor in an ordered confusion of knobbly knees, hobnailed boots, notebooks and pencils. I was wild to experience this marvel and would not believe it when I was assured that I would be unable to understand the lessons; so I was allowed to sit in on one. It took only a few minutes before I had to be removed, near to tears with boredom and chagrin – the Grown-Ups were right, but how I hated having to admit it! Later came a complicated extension system whereby the lessons could be relayed to the Big Room, and later still the school's own, more up-to-date radio system. The school gardens were not a "first", but they were impressive – little plots at the top of the playground, carefully tilled by the big boys under my mother's supervision. You may ask whether she was qualified in Rural Sciences. The answer is "no". But she held to the old-fashion belief that "A good teacher can teach; the subject matter is immaterial". If you were going to take up school gardening, or poultry- or rabbit-keeping, you read it up and then got on with it. No problem at all. (When she was well past sixty, enjoying some post-retirement teaching in an independent school, she taught herself typing and shorthand so as to teach the Commercial course – no one else would take it on). And her enterprises flourished. Really she loved anything new, as long as it was not labelled "modern methods". The gardens were dug, manured, sown and weeded, and the produce triumphantly taken home in due season. Gardening was the setting of my first experience of children's almost uncanny bilingualism. My mother was discussing with one of the boys the failure of his best marrow to reach maturity. "Yes Governess", "No Governess", I heard, in impeccable style. Then turning to his mates, the official enquiry ended, he commented in broadest Wiltshire "Ar, I did let 'n bide too long, and now the frost 'ave got 'n".

But the poultry-keeping was the real triumph. It stemmed, I think, from our relationship with the farm adjoining the school playground. The farmer's daughter kept her poultry in the field the other side of the school fence – a glorious collection of multi-coloured, multi-breed hens with a lordly, high strutting cockerel in charge. They were a source of endless interest and enjoyment to us; we watched and studied them in the sunshine for hours on end. (When in later years I came across the concept of "pecking order" I realized that I had known it for years – we knew exactly which of Miss Bridgeman's hens were the dominant and quarrelsome ones, which the timid who always got last look in at the feeding trough). Seeing our interest, Miss Bridgeman allowed us to help in collecting the eggs and feeding the chickens. We learned to call them with the traditional cry of "Coup, coup,

coup," to appraise knowingly the points of a good laying hen; and we longed for poultry of our own. I am not sure whether these were achieved first, or the school ones, or both together. But a piece of the field was acquired and fenced in, and work began in earnest. My mother masterminded the operation, with the blessing of the Education Authority – and presumably some initial funds as well. The first poultry house was bought. Other smaller ones were made – planned by the boys to scale and built under "Governess's" supervision. One of the gipsy boys, eager for quick results, queried the necessity of some process or stage in construction. When my mother explained, he shook his head in admiration. "You got the brain, Governess. You really 'ave got the brain".

"And still he gazed, and still the wonder grew
That one small head could carry all she knew."

Accounts were kept. Eggs were sold. Baby chicks were hatched. Surplus stock was killed and sold for the table. There were visits from benign deities of The County, who descended, guided, instructed in the mysteries of preparing birds professionally for the table. "Best dressed chicken" (which now seems to me a rather ambiguous phrase) became a popular class to enter in the village Flower Show. The poultry-keeping flourished for years. I think that it was only the war, rationing poultry food and red-taping the distribution of eggs, which made it too difficult to continue. The rabbit project followed, but was short-lived. I was away at College by then, so know little of it at first hand, but I can swear that it was conducted in the same business-like style – my mother just was like that.

How any human being could be so totally committed to both her school and her family still remains a mystery to me. Maybe Susie, whose life has run along similar lines, is the only one of us who can really understand it. Fortunately, "Governess" was a born and inspired organizer. There was a hallowed institution known as the "School Treat", which involved weeks of preparation and planning. In those days Church schools were subject, once a year, to a Diocesan Examination in Scripture, which meant that an appointed examiner, in our case the vicar of the next parish, visited for a morning to test the children's scriptural knowledge. It was not exactly a dreaded occasion, for he was a kindly and reasonable man (not like one of whom it was said that he complained because the eight-year olds didn't seem to understand the doctrine of the Trinity), but it was still an Occasion. Traditionally, the afternoon was a half-holiday when the children were given tea at the Vicarage, preceded by what we should now call a school sports day. This was an opportunity for physical prowess of every kind – long jump, high jump, leapfrog, pole-vaulting, sack-races, three-legged races, egg-and-spoon races, obstacle races – you name it, they had it. The Infants were not forgotten. My mother excelled in thinking up events for them – a cats' race, in which the course was taken on all fours with the competitors meowing at the tops of their voices, was one of the most popular. There was even a stage when proper sports kit (of the period) was worn – yellow shirts, dark brown decent

knickers for the girls, dark brown shorts for the boys – all made in "Needlework" by the big girls, all worn with pride. Oh, we were a proper school – no doubt about that. Numbers may have been small and outstanding talent rare in consequence – eighty children in total was an amazing peak, sixty was nearer the usual average – but when it came to putting on a show, there was a role for everyone.

I remember other "shows" – concerts given by the whole school, class by class, at one of which I solemnly appeared in a dance as "Spirit of the Dawn", tripping uncertainly, but to my own mind with exquisite grace, across the stage – a section of the Big Room, cleared for the occasion. How vast it looked then – thirty feet long, we were told – the audience sitting on desks and chairs or standing crammed in at the back, the Infant Room given over to props, costumes and changing. I had forgotten, until only recently a happy chance gave me a pile of old Parish Magazines to look through, that I also took the part of a dragon when the Brownies performed "The Dragon Who Liked Cake". And one January there was a Nativity Play, ambitious and impressive, put on by the Guides and Brownies together. It must have had a worldwide flavour, for my part was that of an Indian girl – "Red" Indian I mean – and my costume was a delight both in the making and the wearing, hessian with bold bright wool embroidery, much be-fringed and be-feathered. There were Guide and Brownie parties at Christmas – some held in the school, some in the larger space of the Hut. Each had a theme – fancy dress one year, flower costumes another. My large round glasses must have suggested the fancy dress in which I once appeared. A photograph shows me in a miniature academic gown and mortar-board, smiling owlishly, unconscious of the slightly comic effect of my usual thick socks and heavy shoes below. I remember, too, sewing endless blue crepe paper petals on to

a last year's summer dress, while my mother concocted a beautiful flower headdress for me as "Love-in-a-mist". (With typical childish egocentricity, I find it hard to remember Phil's and Susie's parts in the plays, or their fancy dress or flower costumes). Small presents were given at the parties, always appearing under some unusual guise. The best memory for me is that of the year when my mother made an imitation Loch Ness Monster, who trundled in making a pitiful noise – (this was supplied by a "Ma-ma" voice-box, the last relic of my late lamented doll Edith Pamela). The monster was discovered to be in pain and to need an immediate operation, which of course revealed the presents he had unwittingly swallowed. "Lochy's" pains were alleviated, and as the younger children were collected by their fathers, and the older ones went confidently off into the safe dark evening, frost crackling underneath their boots, all were content. Yes – Governess really 'ad got the brain.

I have already said that we three girls (we were never "the children", always "the girls") entered, left and re-entered this world of the village school. I find my memories very hazy as to the timing and the stages by which this happened. I know that we all partook to some extent of the Infant Room, though we had learned to read long before we got there. I recall happy Infant Room hours spent in the pursuit of "unravelling", when the children were all given little pieces of material to pull apart, carefully, thread by thread. I am still wondering what the educational purpose was, but perversely (children *will* enjoy the wrong things!) I loved it, delighting in the feel of the dark blue silk which I was given, excited as I saw how its colour and texture were created by the black and pale blue of the two sets of threads. But when it came to mastering a weaving process, as opposed to un-weaving, that was difficult – over one, under one, large blunt-ended needle hauling coloured raffia endlessly in and out, round and round, on a little disc of card with edges serrated to keep the criss-crossing strings in place. I was an impatient child, always out for quick results, and I hated it. Hated, too, learning to knit. At home I had dropped my needles down gratings, tangled my grubby bit of knitting hopelessly, in an effort to avoid my mother's instruction. "In, round, through, off" was Greek to me for ages. I can still hear the note of triumph in the Infant Teacher's voice when she reported to my mother "I've got Alison to knit at last." (And the process once mastered, I loved it and still do). It is strange that these memories all cluster round "handwork".

I have a feeling that we by-passed the Junior class. I think that Phil arrived in my mother's Senior class at a phenomenally early age, to be cherished and admired, and that I was there for a short time – or was it only an occasional visit? I sat behind a big girl with a beautiful fat smooth pig-tail, which I just had to pull, gently, at intervals – hard enough for her to turn round and smile indulgently, not often enough to incur "Governess's" wrath. (In school we automatically addressed her as "Governess" like the other children). It was in school too that I used to maintain that I couldn't see the blackboard, and march out to the front of the class to read it. This was at first attributed to my usual "showing-off", but led at last to the discovery of my genuine myopia and the provision of the round glasses which gave me, for the first time, clarity of vision as well as that faintly Professorial look.

I don't think Susie ever reached the Senior class, but it is all, as I have said, very confused. Somewhere above our heads a great debate was going on, and my father won. We were not to go through the normal process of village school, a "scholarship" to a "secondary" or "grammar" school, and so to Training College or University. To his way of thinking all this would involve far too many unknown horrors – too much mixing with the outside world, too early a loosening of family ties, perilous cycle rides to catch equally perilous trains to the nearest possible school in Swindon – no, no, it could not be. He would educate us at home himself. He reckoned that his somewhat peculiar health was quite equal to the task, and his academic standards more than adequate. I conjecture that he must have hated his own schooldays (although he had some interesting tales to tell of them) and was really never aware that a sort of forcing-process at home could involve any kind of deprivation for us. We were all to be teachers – a respectable, totally safe profession. (Little did he foresee how the 1980s were to repeat the sorry tale of the great Depression then only just lifting). We were all to go to the Salisbury Diocesan

Training College, because it was the nearest. We were to be prepared by him as external candidates for the London Matriculation Examination – hereafter reverently alluded to as The Exam – taking sufficient subjects for College entry. And that was that.

I wonder whether, today, he might have been taken to court over it? But as far as I know, "Trowbridge", the local seat of educational government, (the odd disaffected parent had been known to threaten to "write to Trowbridge", but I doubt if they ever did) – Trowbridge couldn't have cared less. I believe that our exercise books were once offered to a visiting Inspector, as proof that we really were being taught, but he couldn't have cared less either. Was there a sudden severance from my mother's school, or was there an interim, in-and-out period when we were now here, now there? I cannot make a coherent account from my own recollections, and I am determined to write from them alone, not checking my memory against Phil's, because I hope that she will one day, independently, write her own account of our shared childhood, and at this stage I don't want us to influence each other even unconsciously. I remember arithmetic and drawing lessons from my mother – at home, not in school; but these did not last long, though her piano lessons went on until we reached the limit of our capacity and in my case, well after that, for I am the poor performer in a family of real talent. I recall seemingly endless handwriting practices; there was the day when, at home, I blew out the candle by which I was to work, hoping at least to postpone the evil, but only gaining a scolding. And the day at school when I had toiled my hardest, trying to make the letters touch the double red and blue lines just as they should. I took my book to the front of the class, thinking happily "Now this time they really will be pleased" (who were "they"? The Infant Teacher? "Governess"?), only to be told as usual "Go back and do it again better". I can still taste the feeling of blank despair that swept over me – how could I do any better? Would "they" never be satisfied? I wonder now whether this was during my pre-glasses period – perhaps I really couldn't see what I was doing? Or was it another of the fruits of my impatience? My writing is still shocking!

I remember, too, a time when it was fun to learn snippets of French from my father – to chant "Un, deux, trois," and sing, parrot-fashion, "Au clair de la lune" and "Sur le pont d'Avignon". Then it came to me that this was happening every day, and looked like going on happening every day. Shades of the prison house indeed! What an unjustifiable interference with the really important things of life, such as watching Miss Bridgeman's chickens, grubbing in my own patch of garden for buried treasure, racing reluctant snails with Phil and

Susie. I kept my indignation to myself, of course – in our family it was simply "not done" to rebel against the fiats of the Grown-Ups, however incomprehensible – and accepted the inevitable. A more or less regular timetable evolved. Apart from the obligatory English, Arithmetic, Algebra and Geometry, my father's gift for languages dictated the rest – French, German and Latin, (the last he learned himself, step by step, one jump ahead of us). He must have had an inkling that this was an unbalanced diet, for books with a bearing on History and Geography began to appear casually, a few of them carrying a small (very small) financial bonus for any who would read, mark, learn, and answer questions on them. Later, London Matriculation syllabuses were studied, old question papers obtained for practice work, set books ordered, and we went through a steaming-up process in which The Exam became the be-all and end-all of our lives.

My father certainly achieved his object. We did all pass our "London Matric." We did all gain our entry to the Salisbury Diocesan Training College, and leave there as qualified teachers after our two-year training – two years which to me at least were probably the happiest, the most stretching and deepening of all my post-childhood life. But I can't recommend the system. Educationalists make much of the need to bring school and home together, but in our case they were far too much together. A child should be able to shake off a bad day in school on going home, but we could not do this. Inevitably we did have the odd bad day when we fell below my father's exacting standards (for he taught with a devastating accuracy and expected the same from us), and tea-time would be a gloomy affair in consequence. The narrowness of our curriculum was a draw-back too, partly remediable and, I hope, remedied, by our own efforts in later life, though I fear that "science" remains a largely closed book to all three of us.

But it was the lack of contact (and competition) with other children that I think was the most to be regretted. Susie and I, especially, used to watch the school playground enviously from our garden path when the children were outside for "drill" and at their playtimes. (Phil must, I think, have incurred more domestic responsibilities than we had by this time, for I can't recall her as a wistful watcher). "Drill" was taken by the Junior teacher, with great panache, in accordance with the official "Handbook of Suggestions" of the period. It may actually have been more fun to watch than to perform, with its precise movements executed to numbers, its smart response to almost military-style commands. "Running on the spot – begin! One, two, one, two…" "Arms bend! Right knee – raise! Lower! Hands on backs of thighs – place!" (very chaste wording, this). Playtimes were a real joy. The older boys went mostly for their own version of football, on a rough piece of the playground reserved for them, though in season peg tops would appear, to be spun and whipped with skill; or "conkers" would absorb them for a few days. But the big girls and the younger children I remember as enacting faithfully a wonderful range of traditional singing games, playing hopscotch as their mothers and grandmothers had done in the same playground before them, turning a long skipping rope to initiate the little ones into the mysteries of "Salt, mustard, vinegar, pepper", the rope turning faster and faster till at "pepper", the winter-booted or summer-"dapped" feet hardly seemed to touch the ground. ("Daps" were what you may know as plimsoles, pumps, tennis shoes or trainers, according to your area and age). The children dashed past our windows when released for play, with joyful shouts of "First! Second! Third!", obviously relishing this little slice of real life inserted into their teacher-planned day. Sometimes we were allowed to join them, but this was a rare treat indeed. Sunday School, the

Choir, Brownie and Guide meetings, became social occasions of great moment – almost the only ones we had.

Our main resources were ourselves and each other, a pool of communal imagination fed by our books, and our native inventiveness – and of course, the wonderful, never-failing natural world around us. Our leisure time decreased as the demands of "lessons" became heavier. We were much too busy to be bored, but we did become quarrelsome at times. I don't know whether I was really the worst offender, but I can recall a period when I seemed to be either fighting Phil because she wanted to "boss" me, or Susie because she wouldn't let me "boss" her. I can only hope, in retrospect, that this period didn't last too long – perhaps it happens in all families, not just in rather isolated ones like ours.

But there were compensations in the gently advancing years, (though to me nothing can be as consciously blissful as being seven years old), with their ordered structure of learning which succeeded the golden age of play, and play only. Our frontiers of independence were gradually pushed a little further out from the home centre. If we could "go to fetch the milk" without Grown-Ups, we could also be allowed short walks without them for our own devices. Thus I was occasionally allowed to walk up the Hill after school with my "best friend" of the Brownies (and later, of the Guides and Choir) and maintain a tenuous but happy relationship with her which lasted over a good few years. She was the almost perfect friend who demanded nothing, and accepted without fuss any slivers of time and companionship which I was able to give, and I remember her with affection and gratitude. We grabbed at all the time outside "lessons" which we could still call our own, revelled in the unplanned hours of weekends and holiday times. We had to pay lip-service to the Grown-Up dictum that "lessons" were all-important, but secretly we knew better. Some philosopher has defined education as "that which is left when you have forgotten all that you learned at school". Maybe that is on the cynical side, and I am grateful for much of my father's rigorous teaching; but looking back, I am sure that my real education took place less in than out of school.

---

* Mrs Pringle was the formidable school cleaner in "Miss Read's" village school.

In a sense, time does not exist for the first two or three years of one's life. A small child lives in an infinite Now, with no beginning, no end in sight. Wholly given over to the experience or the emotion of the moment, you take thought for neither yesterday nor tomorrow. But the conventional sequencing of time soon enough begins to order your days, parcelling them out in an orderly fashion with time to get up, breakfast time, dinner time, tea time, bed time, you won't have time for that, yes, when I have time I'll make your doll a pair of knickers. Weeks slide into shape – so many school days followed by a glorious Saturday and Sunday – then group themselves into months. The chanting of "January, February, March, April, May..." or "Thirty days hath September..." as well as being an achievement is a useful device to keep them in place. But years! They are totally unmanageable monsters, first dimly apprehended, perhaps, as the vast space in between one's birthdays (at five one can scarcely accept the possibility of ever really being six), or the awful yawning gap between this Christmas and the next. I remember a feeling of real desolation when the Christmas tree, browning and dropping its needles, was carried outside, our Christmas presents became part of our normal stock-in-trade, and the decorations were carefully put away "ready for next year". Our young Christmases were such festivals of glitter and goodwill, paper chains and presents, that to put one of them behind was almost unbearable, and the promise of "next year" seemed something as unattainable as the moon.

If Christmas was indeed a watershed in our lives, surely it is the point at which I should start to sketch the cycle of a year in my childhood. Preparations began well before the twenty-fifth of December. Perhaps the earliest stirring was my father's annual letter to Bumpus of Oxford Street, ordering "Christmas books" on approval. There would be a special grocery order for the ingredients of the Christmas pudding and mince pies, and the magnificent cake which my mother always produced, despite the vagaries of the oven on the ageing paraffin cooker. Exotic annual delicacies were ordered too – figs, dates and grapes ("Ooh, wipes" once exclaimed an ecstatic small Susie, remembering only dimly the glories of last year). An old boiling fowl, or two as our size and consumption increased, must be ordered from one of the farms. My mother must plan and make her annual shopping expedition to Swindon – somehow my awareness of this co-existed happily for years with a belief in Father Christmas. As we grew older, presents all round the family must be concocted, as secretly as possible. My father's time-honoured joke that his favourite colour was purple with a green edge was worked assiduously into pen-wipers, razor towels, notebooks, anything we could devise. Later, when the Bus had begun to run, we would be allowed to accompany my mother on it for a joint shopping spree. Two shillings spent at Woolworths (still in those days with nothing over sixpence, and most things far less) would yield all the presents we girls needed to buy, chosen with infinite care and deliberation. Why did I, one year, decide that an oil lamp some six inches high – a real oil lamp –was the very thing for Susie, while she, circling Woolworths independently, decided on the very same thing for me? We treasured those little lamps for years.

My mother's cookery must have been carried out largely after we were in bed, at least for our earliest Christmases which were the most glorious of all. Stirring the pudding was a ritual which I well remember. The boiling fowl or fowls would be fetched from the farm, either by my mother on her bicycle, or later by the three of us. No oven-ready poultry in those days! They had to be plucked and drawn, a process which Susie and I loved to watch, but which Phil hated and shunned. What a thrill when, one year, the farmer must have misjudged and killed a bird in full lay, for she was found to contain an egg, hard-shelled and complete, as well as others in varying stages of development. Into the stuffing it went, with many compliments to the thoughtfulness of the bird! Steamed before roasting, the fowls after their free-ranging life had a tenderness and flavour far beyond the mass-produced, cage-reared objects of today. Now that chicken is the cheapest kind of weekend joint, it is hard to believe that it was beyond our family pocket except as a Christmas treat.

Somehow then, with much literal burning of midnight oil, the cooking was done. Christmas Eve arrived. This was the day for a short walk with my father to collect branches of yew which would later be skilfully arranged to make a Christmas Tree. The family stock of paper chains would be ceremonially brought down from a minute box-room (where apples still lay in rows if it was a good year), and fastened up in their appointed, traditional places. The tree would not be decorated till we were in bed – and we would willingly go early, as all children do on Christmas Eve, each hanging up one of my father's home-knitted socks. As he was six feet three tall, with a length of foot to match, they were excellent for the purpose. Not once, though a poor sleeper, did I hear "Father Christmas" creep in to remove and fill the stockings and put them back. But he must have done, for full they were in the morning. The

first of us awake was allowed to wake the others, and the rifling of stockings began. Heavy and lumpy, we knew that they would contain an apple and an orange, a carefully wrapped mince pie, and a few miscellaneous small things – enough to content us while our parents caught up on a few hours' well earned sleep. Then, up! "Merry Christmas" all round the family! and the thrill of coming downstairs to the chain-hung living-room, where the tree now stood resplendent with its tinsel and glittering ornaments, and real candles waiting to be lit in the evening; and underneath it, the three piles of presents, to be opened after a special Christmas breakfast of poached eggs.

The whole day shone. Words cannot convey the sheer enchantment of it all. I don't remember a time when we did not know the true reason for Christmas, even before "going to church" became an indispensable part of the day. Peace and goodwill flowed around like a warm golden river, so that it seemed impossible that one would ever fight one's sisters, or argue with one's parents, again. Everyone's presents were always "exactly what I wanted". On one occasion when Phil, with unwonted daring, had crept downstairs to look at the presents under the tree, telling Susie and me when we woke that she had dreamed what we were all going to have, (and we innocents believed her), it was only an additional thrill. We lost ourselves in new toys, new books, surfacing only when the Christmas dinner, the feast of the year, was announced, and later, tea with the Christmas cake which we were almost too surfeited to want, but which we annually pronounced to be "the best you've ever made". When dark fell, the candles would be lit on the tree, making it a blaze of loveliness with every ornament gleaming and sparkling in the soft flickering light. Today's fairy lights are pretty (and probably much safer), but they cannot touch real candles. Later, we would all sit round while my mother started the annual reading aloud of Dickens' "Christmas Carol", which ushered in her reading of our new Christmas books. Nobody seemed to care what time we went to bed, so the magic of the day was prolonged, till eventually we yielded to sleepiness, with the prospect of more magical days ahead, when time would not exist and toys would still be new.

How well I remember some of those toys! Often there were new dolls, for although active, open-air children we were also very doll-minded. Indeed as the years went on, the dolls, teddy bears and other animals became a considerable collection, carefully arranged in families in the big cot vacated by its last inhabitant, Susie, and filling it to over-flowing. Each new doll had to be named, and there was much heart searching before the right name (usually rather high-flown) was found. Today, if you ask a small child her doll's name, more often than not you will get a blank stare, or the reply "Dolly", "Baby", or "Tiny Tears". But I had Josephine, Lucy, Olive, Edith Pamela (I thought Pamela was a surname), and others – all with personalities to match their names. One Christmas brought a little bird, plush-covered, which hopped round in circles when wound up. I loved that bird and had him for many, many years. Another, shorter-lived mechanical toy was a humming-top. It fascinated my father, and he played with it solidly all Christmas Day and Boxing Day till the mechanism rebelled and broke. In compensation I was allowed to choose another toy of the same value from Gamages' catalogue (which always came to us, but was seldom used except for cutting-out purposes). I chose a nice little sack of coloured wooden bricks, with which I was well content, and the humming-top episode became a piece of family history. There was the Christmas when our main presents were combined to produce a set of Meccano – and, the biggest surprise of all in my memory, the scooter Christmas. We had picked up vague hints and thought that there might, just might, be a scooter for us all to share – but under the tree stood three...... I think words failed us at such incredible bounty. There were always the new books too, but they must have later space to themselves.

The glorious, unplanned days after Christmas flew by. All too soon came that desolation of Christmas over, and the rhythm of school, one way or another, began to rule our days again. And now it would seem that winter began in earnest.

There would be weeks when we were virtually confined to the house by rain or snow, and it became, alas, perfectly feasible to fight one's sisters again. I don't suppose that our childhood winters were either as constantly wet, or as snowy, as I remember them, any more than the summers were all hot. But in the country you are very close to the weather in all its intensity; there is no escaping it, or its consequences. February really seemed to be a fill-dyke month, and I thought it was hard luck on Phil to have her birthday at such a miserable time of the year, even though the first snowdrops would be visible to greet her. Thick white chalky mud caked our wellington boots after the necessary forays outside to fetch the milk or feed the chickens. We had constant colds, and chilblains on our feet. Poor Susie had them on her little blue hands as well. But you did not expect, as one does now, to be warm in the winter. Our "Valor Perfection" oilstoves, moved from room to room as required, mitigated the chill of the stone walls, but that was about all. It was all we expected, anyway; we piled on layers of clothes and got on with living. Bed time was a particularly chilly business. Hot water bottles were a luxury used only if you were ill. You undressed, or were undressed, rapidly, after a minimal wash in the kitchen (country school houses had no bathrooms!), jumped quickly into a cold bed and thawed it, shudderingly, yourself. If it was really Arctic weather, though, our bedroom might have been warmed beforehand by one of the oilstoves. We would plead to have it left for a little while after we were in bed and the candle was blown out – not for warmth, but for the delight of watching the lovely flickering patterns of light which its perforated top threw on to the ceiling. For all of us, this is a much cherished recollection.

There would be days of snow, sometimes days on end of snow. We always knew if it had snowed in the night by the muffling of footsteps in the lane outside and the strange light effect through our bedroom curtains. Small amounts of snow meant fun and games outside; meant soaked woolly gloves dripping on the guard round the oilstove, and cold hands driving me indoors while Phil and Susie (despite her chilblains) were still cavorting outside. Deep snow meant confinement, meant Grown-Up anxiety as to whether the Bread and the Meat would get through (they nearly always did), meant only a handful of children in school, steaming out around the roaring Tortoise stove. We envied my father, impervious to cold outside – in his heyday he would go striding off for long walks in the snow, coming back with amazing accounts of drifts as high as himself. Our white cat leapt unwillingly through the miniature snowdrifts in the garden, dingy and grubby, an affront to the dazzling purity around him. With all its inconveniences, the snow never failed to excite and exhilarate, and to this day I still catch my breath in wonder at the first fall.

There were frosty spells too – days of biting cold and hard ground, from which, as we grew older, one of us had to prise out reluctant leeks or Jerusalem artichokes for the day's quota of vegetables – a job I loathed, especially the artichokes, with poor half-frozen worms embedded in the heavy soil that clung fast to their knobbly shapes. Or there might be brussels sprouts to pick, with numb fingers barely able to dislodge them from their stalks. Vegetables don't come much fresher than that! There were days when our walk to fetch the milk was a procession of delight under hoar-frosted trees against a blue sky, and we lingered, in spite of the cold, over the beauties of spiders' webs, wild strawberry leaves, even wire-netting, made exquisite by a frosty lace edging.

And then, almost imperceptibly, the winter would loosen its grip. There would come odd days when the stirring of Spring could be felt, as well as seen in the springing of green shoots under hedges. We hailed the first celandine or pink dead-nettle; even the groundsel which we would later have to pull out as a troublesome weed was welcomed when it first showed its scrubby yellow flower-head. Came days of light wind and wild sunshine, when we pleaded to go out in the garden without our coats, unable to bear their constricting warmth any longer, feeling the madness of Spring in every fibre of our being. We laughed, shouted, leaped, ran, re-discovered every corner of our little domain. Under the elder hedge between our garden and the school playground we poked and grubbed in the now loose earth released from the frost. We revelled in its gritty freshness, in the exciting small treasures it threw up – "special" stones, bits of coloured china, a piece of glass which Susie, digging for moles (why moles?) mistook excitedly for the twinkle in her quarry's eye. Our young sharp senses registered the distinctive smells of the good fresh earth, the broken elder twigs or ivy trails (quite different), the brilliant springing green nettles trodden under our feet and avoided, if possible, by our hands. If one was stung, the country remedy of dock-leaves (another distinctive smell) was always at hand; crushed and rubbed on to the stung spot, mixed with a little spit, they at least tempered the first vicious smart. And over all the sun, the intoxicating sun! It searched out nuances of colour in every bare twig, gleamed on the polished dark ivy leaves, glanced off golden straws or the brittle dead silver stems of last year's flowers. Spring-crazy, chattering starlings shone, their neat sober feather suits transformed for once into the greens and blues of the hopeful illustrations in my "ABC of Birds". The burnished bronze cock, scarlet-combed, lording it over Miss Bridgeman's flock of glistening hens, became (and he knew it) a very prince of poultry. The light wind wafted the scents and sounds of the country to us as we played – the good sweet smell of milky cows mingling healthily with whiffs of farmyard manure, the contented croodling (my mother's word) of the hens forming a background to their excited cackling triumphant announcement of another egg laid, the arrogant crowing of the cock. It relayed the clang of churns and buckets at milking time, the lowing of the contented cows, the thin bleat of lambs from the fields on top of the Hill. No matter if that same wind later brought clouds and a little rain – it was a gentle Spring rain which we could welcome at the end of an ecstatic day of sensuous, almost animal joy. You must have felt the rigours of Winter really bite you, if you are to deserve the intoxicating advent of Spring.

The days lengthened, softened. The garden clamoured for attention and was put in order, with increasing help from "the girls" as we grew older. I cannot remember not gardening, from the earliest grubbing days onwards to real help and responsibility. It was a season of "firsts" – first primrose, violet, cowslip. First piece of pale blue starling's egg to be

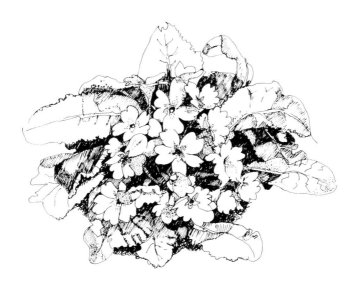

picked up – sign that baby birds were beginning to hatch – to be followed by the deeper blue of the thrush's egg, the blotched turquoise of the blackbird's. First acquaintance with death, perhaps, in the pathetic little naked corpses, blob-eyed, huge triangular beaks gaping, of the babies that fell from their nests under our roof. At first we buried each one tenderly, but later we would lose interest. Three hawthorn trees stood on the outer edge of the school playground, one "belonging" to each of us. Whose tree would first show the tight green buds which country children nibble, calling them "bread and cheese"? (I loved to do this, and had to be bound by a solemn promise not to experiment with the nibbling of other, potentially poisonous buds and leaves). First house-martins to arrive, twittering ecstatically, skimming their lovely unmistakable flight round the church tower and over the school roof, dipping to find the shells of last year's nests waiting to be re-built. First cuckoo's song – but you had to be very sure about this; children in the country love to mimic the cuckoo. We expected both house martins and cuckoo punctually on the sixteenth of April, and were rarely disappointed; and Phil, keeper of meticulous Nature records for years, could probably give you the usual dates for all the other "firsts" as well.

Into this burst of new life and growth everywhere, Easter slotted naturally, though in our early years it was less of a festival than Christmas. It was understood that Easter eggs were not to be expected – if they appeared it was a bonus, indicating a slight temporary upturn in family finances. When we reached our early teens, and Confirmation had admitted us to the full joys of Easter – only then did we begin to understand something of it.

Good Friday, after church services, would be primrosing day, when, fortified with three hot cross buns in a paper bag, we would set out to gather the lovely fragrant things from sunny banks and hedgerows, ready for the decorating of the church on Saturday. We picked and picked, tying the bunches with wool as we went; it was not despoiling (as such picking would be in these days of herbicides and "efficient" farming), for there was primrose bounty enough and to spare. On Easter Sunday we would recognize our bunches, on windowsills or round the font, adding their gentle praise to the glory of the daffodils and narcissus from the Vicarage garden which crowded the church, shouting Alleluias from golden trumpets. I have no words to convey the feeling of a village Easter, the wonderful sense of the unity of all creation as the choir led the familiar Easter hymns and the flowers joined in giving glory to the Lord of Life. Easter, Spring, Resurrection – the flowers, the bread and the wine – all fused into one timeless, yet everyday miracle.

So Easter gained in radiance, a quality of joy later apprehended than the homeliness of Christmas. Joy continued to flow as the Spring advanced towards Summer. Late Spring storms enhanced it, by contrast, the beauty of the season, rather than marring it. My heart leapt when, twenty years on, I found that someone else had experienced storms as I had, and had caught the experience as I could not –

INVITATION AFTER THE STORM

What change one hour can bring!
Come out and see narcissus bow again
Their innocent pale faces after rain
And stare in purity at calm, pearled grass.
Listen, the wrenchings of your window cease,
And with a soft, enormous sound of peace,
The winds, unangered, through your tall trees pass,
The washed birds sing.

And how the washed birds did sing! How the bluebells and narcissus in our front garden drank in the warm Spring rain, and the wet lilac bushes which were our front hedge raised their bowed heavy clusters of dripping pink or white fragrance into the sunshine again, while tiled roofs steamed and children watched the puddles dry underfoot.

And everywhere went on the seasonal round of work in farm, garden and allotment, the countryfolks' ageless wisdom timing each process in the cycle of birth and germination; nothing rushed or fussed, everything to its own season. We absorbed the rhythm, felt the rightness of each task we saw in progress as the year brought it round again. But there was one which we greeted with particular eagerness. We would wake early on some warm morning, hearing the insistent cuckoo mingle his song with the pert chirping of the sparrows outside our window and the metallic shirring, shrilling sound of the starlings, varied by a few bars of mimicked blackbird's song or woodpecker's yaffle, for starlings are clever birds. We would register, almost unconsciously, all the familiar sounds of our household coming to life. Then a distant noise, strange and yet dimly remembered, gaining in volume till it drowned our excited voices and fading away again, would give the signal. The hay-cutter had rattled its way along the lane to start work. This really meant summer! It meant air fragrant with the smells of cut grass and drying hay. It meant a feeling of tension over the whole village – would the weather hold till the cut hay had been dried, turned, dried again, and was safely brought in to the farmyard in lumbering, creaking wooden hay wagons, to be stacked there ensuring next winter's cattle feed? More immediately, please may we put on our summer dresses today? And shall we be taken to play in a hayfield – to fling the fragrant stuff at each other, build houses and nests with it, get hayseeds down our backs and in our sandals, see how the grass springs again the day after it is cut? Oh, hay is a wonderful experience. I have even (praise be!), later in childhood, helped to harvest it from a small field by hand, raking the dry swathes into "cocks" with a wooden hayrake, pitchforking it into the wagons, joining the triumphant jolt back to the farm with the huge cushion of hay bouncing deliciously beneath me and the race against gathering black clouds only just won. What happiness, what basic goodness of life has been mine.

One thing only we now need to complete the coming of Summer. After the Spring "first" flowers come the Summer ones. Bluebells and campions have already mingled with the white froth of the cow-parsley which we have not yet learned to call "Queen Ann's Lace", and which I refuse to call "keck". As the bluebells fade, we wait and watch for the flower which has become our summer flower above all others, and which to me now *is* my country childhood – the meadow cranesbill. Suddenly it is everywhere, great clumps filling the grassy

verges of the lanes, pink-tinged stems with downy spreading leaves upholding the wonderful, indescribably blue flowers. Once in bloom it will go on all the summer; even when the grass verges are mown by the roadman with his sweeping scythe, it will spring again, this time having a chance to form the pointed seedheads which give it its name. This is the flower for which I have pined when away from my native chalk soil, which makes the lanes a hazy dream of beauty and assures us that all is well with our world. Now Summer can flaunt all her other riches in their rightful places, for the Queen of the summer flowers is reigning at last, and our cup runneth over.

Looking back, it seems that one sunny day just followed another, and that all our childhood summers were spent in the ecstatic enjoyment of the outdoor world. It hardly matters whether this is "true" or not, when one is aiming to recapture the gold and leave the dross. I must be looking back to days before "school" when our garden, plus the school playground when the children had vacated it, held all that we needed to absorb us throughout the golden sunlit hours. A rough grass plot was given over to a sturdy swing, a hammock and a tent, leaving ample space in between for the outdoor meals which my mother taught us to love, though my father preferred the comfort of "indoors". We would troop up the garden path with plates of bread and butter, dishes of our own lettuce ("don't forget the salt"), bowls of raspberries or currants from our own bushes, the jam, the milk, the lot – even plates of liver and bacon on Fridays when the butcher had called. One of us must stay to keep insects away from the feast which they were anxious to share. How many times Phil was stung while rescuing ungrateful, jammy wasps from the little blue jam pot (for her tender but tenacious spirit refused to have them killed), I dread to think. Last would come my mother with a huge and comfortable brown tea pot...... Never has food tasted better.

This grass plot was the scene of many activities. Especially blissful were the days when my mother filled the old galvanized baby bath with water and put it out for us to splash and dabble in. We sailed boats; drowned small dolls; turned the bath into a lily-pool, with buttercups pushed through the centres of plantain leaves to make the water lilies. We helped to cut the grass with garden shears and made our own private haystack. We sorrowed over the snails on which we trod, accidentally, with horrid crunching and squelching of remains, and lovingly cherished others in jam jars, feeding them with nice fresh dandelion leaves. But they were uncooperative pets, always escaping, unwilling to race when asked, the larger ones reluctant to draw matchbox sledges out of which the tinies climbed as fast as they could go. We eyed the fruit on the raspberry bushes that bordered one side of the plot, and the currant and gooseberry patch on the other, waiting for the time of plenty when we would be allowed to pick and eat at will – till then, fruit-picking to order was a chore. We had huge dolls' tea parties, bringing out our entire stock to make a really imposing array. It must have been after one of these that I went to bed leaving a little soft doll, Winnie, (podgy, with dark hair and a pale green dress) outside in punishment for some misdemeanour she had committed, heedless of my mother's warning that the night dew would ruin her. Later I was overcome by remorse – how unkind I had been to poor Winnie, who probably knew no better anyway! How could I possibly abandon her to the unknown terrors of a night outside? In real distress I called down to my mother and begged her to bring Winnie in. Whether in fact she had already done so I never knew – but the occasion remains vividly in my memory as the first stirring of a real conscience, quite a different thing from being adjudged "naughty" by a Grown-Up.

In the middle of the summer beauty came my birthday, with special flowers -- red roses, delphiniums, and Madonna lilies – picked for me and arranged always in the same glass jug. Birthdays meant happiness, everyone at their best, a modest sort of present and one of my mother's superb cakes. Mine, being the only summer birthday, was marked by attempts at a "proper" picnic, further afield than the grass plot, but July is a chancy month and I don't think the picnic often materialized – instead there grew up a family legend to the effect that it always rains on Alison's birthday. It did not seem to matter; birthdays still had a magical quality, whatever the weather. Presents from one's sisters were apt to have a very homemade, even makeshift character, but were none the less welcome. One's "proper" present was always a thrill, sometimes a surprise. One year I had asked for, and received, a wooden hoop – but as it cost less than the usual present allowance, I also netted the surplus ninepence, laid out on the table in a semi-circle of pennies with the verse

"Presented to you by M. and D.,
Eight whole pennies and one pennee".
This we all thought very witty, especially as it was composed by my father. (My mother was the acknowledged family Laureate, while my father put pen to paper rarely and reluctantly). It was my mother who supplied my biggest ever birthday thrill, though, one year when my present was a collection of the small wild animal figures which Woolworths made so well. Overnight, she arranged them on a table covered with sand (on a sheet of brown paper), with stones from the garden making caves and rocks, and small bushy pieces of ivy for vegetation. It was a lovely miniature desert scene, totally unexpected – and the most amazing thing of all

was that she had used the Front Room table! I was breathless, and could hardly bear to disturb the layout even to play with it; and it was days before I would agree to dismantle it. I wonder now, did she know what a vision of delight she gave me? I hope so – how I hope so.

Hard on my birthday followed the school holidays, which even prior to the establishing of our programme of regular lessons meant six weeks of relaxed routine, and the complete freedom of the school playground. There would be tasks in which we shared when old enough – catching up on gardening, sometimes re-decorating in the house. (Candles, oil lamps and oilstoves soon darken walls and ceilings). I remember one year joyfully helping to pull the wallpaper from our damp bedroom walls – that is, all that was left, for our small restless fingers had stripped some of it, illegitimately, by degrees already. Freshly distempered walls led, one year, to new curtains; my mother's indispensable sewing machine whirred away while one of us turned the handle, a much coveted privilege. But there would also be great tracts of time at our own disposal, time for sheer idleness, for just "being", even for rare moments of solitude. I loved to escape to the edge of our territory, where beyond the school garden plots a telegraph pole, weathered to a silvery mauve colour, hummed gently, and the turf of the bordering field ran over a yard or so on our side of the wire fence. To lie flat on this warm turf in the sunshine, breathing in its faintly aromatic, earthy smell – to watch dreamily its tiny insect inhabitants busily going about their private lives but momentarily impinging on mine – to feel the very heartbeat of the earth beneath me, while one hand on the base of the warm, dry, splintery telegraph pole tingled faintly with its vibrations – this seemed the ultimate bliss of summer. The swallows skimmed, swooped and twittered overhead, sleepy farmyard sounds drifted over to me, the blue sky above was almost too bright to look at. For brief but infinitely suspended seconds I was one with the chalky soil under the turf; I crept with the insects, flew with the swallows, fused with the warmth of the sun. Then thud, thud, thud, amplified by my ear pressed to the ground would come sisterly footsteps, and I would be claimed by Phil or Susie for the next eager ploy, or merely harried on principle away from my moment of solitude, as noisy in participation or protest as any small girl could be.

There was a summer when, with a little Grown-Up help only, we built a shelter from branched sticks (pea sticks?), interwoven, or rather perhaps interstuffed, with bunches of hay from the grass plot, and made it a semi-private, blissful, earwiggy headquarters for all our other activities. There might be a major walk or two. In addition to the short walks which we often enjoyed with my father, and the daily fetching of the milk, we had some grand family expeditions beyond the boundaries of our own village, exploring distant hamlets or locating ancient hill forts, my father carrying a great basket of flasks and sandwiches as if it were a feather. Earlier, I think, was the era of the annual day trip to Weston-super-Mare on an excursion train, an event absolutely bursting with the thrills of the unaccustomed. We would be called before sunrise (so it seemed) to start the journey, by pony-trap or later by the village taxi, to the nearest station, where we boarded the train – mostly in excited silence, though my chattering tongue might have to be hushed by admonitions not to show off. Then, the rattling through the quiet countryside – the plume of white smoke from the good old steam engine, with its glorious smell (never mind the smuts), the plunge into darkness at the Box Tunnel, and finally the arrival! We had buckets and spades. We clambered over rocks, gathered lengths of bladdered seaweed like leathery necklaces, to take home and "pop" by degrees. You could forecast the weather by it, they said. We rode on donkeys. We had a stupendous meal at a café – fish and chips, pink ice cream in shell-shaped glass dishes – sitting grandly on pink wickerwork chairs at a glass-topped table, on our very best behaviour. We even had, incredibly, a little money to spend as we liked. I remember once opting for an extra donkey ride, with the warning that "You'll have nothing left to spend in the shops, and you won't like that". But I stuck to my guns, thought the donkey ride was worth it, and enjoyed the feeling of having made my very own, different choice. It was at Weston, another year, that I bought Dulcima, a rather gaudy celluloid duck who captured my heart and who had three halfpence knocked off her price for my special benefit, the gap between tenpence-halfpenny and a shilling being unbridgeable. Dulcima seemed a vision of beauty at the time and remained a favourite for years. And the sea? Always capricious at Weston, it might be no more than an unattainable silver ribbon, a mile of mud away. Or again, we might be lucky with the tide and be able to paddle – PADDLE! The family photograph album records some of the joys of Weston, my mother decorously hatted, my father looking, as he usually did in photographs, faintly uncomfortable, and the three of us carefully posed, with our straight hair blowing in the wind and all heaven in our eyes.

I never quite knew why these annual expeditions came to an end. Did rail fares go up? But in those days prices were unchanging for years on end. Did family finances just become unequal to the strain, as we grew older and presumably more expensive? Did my father, always a shrinker from humanity in bulk, begin to find it too much to contemplate? At all events, the Weston era ended, and "the seaside" became a memory not to be revived till, in our early teens, the Choir and Sunday School outing swept us luxuriously by coach to Bournemouth. We did not actively resent the end of the trips, or plead for one more – that was not in our family code of behaviour. Years later I learned that Phil had been immensely relieved, for she had been told that as a privilege, "next year" she should take the money to the ticket office and get the tickets. The prospect of this intended treat petrified her, and when "next year" brought no trip to Weston, she felt it was an almost miraculous deliverance. "Si la jeunesse savait" is all very well, but "la viellesse" as represented by the best-intentioned Grown-Ups, can slip up pretty badly at times...

The seasons are always on the move. Even in August there would be mornings which were Autumn's forerunners – chilly mornings wrapped in white mists, giving way to days whose still generous warmth had an indefinable but definite autumnal quality, faintly resented. Berries began to colour up on the wayfaring-tree and guelder-rose, far too early. Bonfire smoke, fragrant but heralding the turn of the year, drifted across the village in the evenings. Cornfields would be ripe for harvest now – climax of the year's cycle of ploughing, sowing and harrowing, reward for all the patient and anxious tending of the crops from slender green blade through to the pale gold of whispering barley and oats and the deep proud gold of the wheat. Reaping was done by a horse-drawn machine whose complexity filled us with amazement, for as it went, it bound the cut corn into sheaves and ejected them in its wake; men and boys plodded behind to set the sheaves up in stooks for final drying. The landscape lay chequered in the sunshine, green fields alternating with the golden stretch of cornfields patterned by the march of the orderly stooks, poppies flaring up from the stubble. Anxious days, till the full sheaves were ready to be tossed into the wagons and jolted to the safety of the farmyard! Then, the thrilling arrival of the threshing machine, drawn from farm to farm by the traction engine that powered it, with gleam of brass and heady whiff of steam!

The corn harvest was in. Suddenly the freedom of the fields carefully skirted for nearly a year was ours to enjoy. We ran exultantly over the cut stubble, glorying in the sense of space, heedless of the straws that poked into our sandals and scratched our bare legs. Susie and I, in a Red Indian phase, found a ready-made prairie in the field at the top of the garden and whooped and cavorted there in our homemade Red Indian suits, with bows and arrows fashioned from sticks from the elder hedge. Miss Bridgeman's hens would be transported to temporary quarters in newly harvested fields, there to live freely and fatly for several weeks on the remnants of the corn. We missed their crowing, cackling, croodling proximity and would walk down to visit them in their holiday resort. But already the days were noticeably shorter, and the evenings were cool.

As the dusk drove us indoors, my father, unwilling perhaps to acknowledge the signs of departing summer, would endlessly prolong his self-appointed task of filling and lighting the oil lamps, so that we would be sitting, resigned or mutinous, in total darkness before the ritual was completed. First the filling; then the match to the upturned wick – is it even, or does it need trimming? Now the tall glass "chimney", polished clean with a dry cloth, is slipped over to enclose the flame, the wick turned low while the chimney warms up. Then at last, after much adjustment and readjustment, the opaque round globe is carefully placed over the chimney, diffusing the welcome, gentle light for which we have been waiting. "The Shadow of Light!" we chant joyfully, taking our places round the pool of visibility cast on the table while the corners of the living room remain in near darkness. Now we can read, knit dolls' clothes, embroider, play Snap or Lexicon, in the time still left before bed.

It is the season now for the country pleasures of blackberries and mushrooms, the former an ungrudged bounty everywhere, the latter attended by a spice of risk, as some farmers resented the intrusion of mushroom pickers into their fields. Of course we knew where the best of each were to be found. We roamed happily over nearby pastures where the blackberries were thick and luscious, filling our paper bags, emptying them into my mother's central, newspaper-lined basket, begging the loan of my father's walking stick to hook down those "best" clusters always just out of reach. Scratches were inevitable and accepted as part of the game. Hands and mouths were stained purple, and our oldest dresses, donned for the occasion, rarely escaped damage. Through the blackberry tangles pushed up golden heads of ragwort and great magenta thistles, topped by intoxicated butterflies so intent on their orgy of nectar that one could view them almost nose-close. There might be a bonus in the form of some rare flower, or glimpse of animal or bird behaviour. Innocent rabbits, who never dreamed of the cruel future horrors of myxomatosis, scampered away at our approach. Could that rather large hole be a fox's earth? Oh, please may I take home that tiny bleached skull (Mole? Vole? Baby rabbit?) – it's perfectly clean...... Wandering, gathering, seeing, is the best part of blackberrying; the next stage, picking over the berries at home, is a tedious one, but the end products are worth it every time – jam and jelly, pies and puddings. Especially puddings.

Mushrooming was my father's great joy, an operation in which he was the commandant and we were valued aides. His tallness and keen sight were great assets. He would stride over the dewy fields, eyes everywhere, and point with his stick to tell-tale gleams of white, while we three, strategically strung out, ran to investigate. We distinguished unerringly between real mushrooms and other fungi, inedible or even dangerous. Puff balls were locally considered highly poisonous, so we stamped on them for the protection of later, possibly less knowledgeable mushroomers, feeling public-spirited and superior. Field mushrooms are beautiful things. Pearly white domes push up through the fine new grass after haycutting, or the best dunged patches of pasture fields, with pinky-brown exquisitely formed gills beneath and a wholesome, earthy mushroom smell for final identification. Mushrooms were really something in those days! One alone would often more than fill our cupped hands as we ran to add it to the store in my father's deep basket. We were taught to leave the tiny "buttons" to grow for another day. Once we found a "horse mushroom" as country people call it, the size of a dinner plate, tasty and tender. There would be bonuses as in blackberrying, like the rare meadow saffron we once found; and also the spice of danger – would we meet the farmer? Only on one occasion did this happen, when we were exploring some new fields (never again!). We stood in embarrassed silence while my father was reproved for trespassing, offered the basketful to the farmer, was refused but warned off for the future. Strangely, the deepest impression I carried away was that of the farmer's shoes – brown shoes! How odd, for my father always wore black, and I thought all men must do the same. Even on this sad occasion there was triumph over the booty. Back at home, we would all sit down to skin the mushrooms, which my mother cooked in milk with a little butter and served on toast. Ravenous after our expedition, we ate them by the plateful, incredulous, but accepting, that my mother "preferred" just to have the dark milky juice, globules of golden butter afloat, on her toast. In later, slightly more affluent years, away from our green pastures but able to afford to buy mushrooms, I noticed that she ate them with as much relish as anyone else…

I have learned to accept the plaints of both parents and children these days that the school holidays are too long and "the kids are bored stiff". I can only listen with shocked pity. With no television, no pocket money, no transport but our own sturdy legs, we never found the holiday long enough. My happy, early memories are of day after day of sunshine, when we played dressed only in short knickers, and you stole a march on your sisters, if possible, by stealthily pulling them on under the bedclothes and then leaping out of bed, whipping off your nightdress and appearing fully dressed – FIRST! There must have been rainy days, of course, but with our books, our doll families, and our purposeful fingers which, under my mother's guidance, were always making something, the wet days passed almost unnoticed. All too soon it would be "school next week", though my father might bountifully grant us (and himself) an extra week's grace. But with the starting again of the "lessons" routine, the summer, we knew, was as good as gone.

Autumn saw the picking and storing of our apple crop, mostly from one amazing tree, variety unknown, whose green-to-golden fruit was sharp and delicious to eat, and cooked to fluffy perfection. The neat rows of apples on top of the old trunks in our tiny box-room were flanked by the huge marrows which were my father's pride, but which we privately thought stringy and unappetizing after a few weeks' storage. It was time for a re-assessment of our own growth, when pleasure in the inches added over the summer mingled with tut-tutting at the implications of new winter clothes needed. My mother would have been knitting the annual quota of socks, grey for us and "heather mixture" for my father, all through the summer. She performed prodigious feats of altering, re-making and letting down. There was the year when scarlet woollen capes, which we had worn with a Red Riding Hood effect when smaller, were made into warm skirts. Unfortunately my father now thought them "too bright", so attempts were made to dye them navy blue. The final result was a rather dingy beetroot colour, which with grey cable-knit jerseys, was certainly sober enough to please anyone; we hated them, but they had to be worn. Last year's warm woolly vests, also hand-knitted by my mother, would be reviewed, lengthened, the worn parts re-knitted. There would be a few unavoidable buys – shoes, a new coat for Phil, warm knickers (little bloomers with a pocket for your hankie on one leg). As we grew older there was less homemade and more bought – plaid skirts in one year, navy blue box-pleated "gym slips" another, with flowered pinafores on top to keep them clean because they don't wash. There was a faint sense of preparation for a siege – the age-old siege of winter – even if it was only felt in the area of clothes. The oilstove would be lit in the evenings, and the school cleaner, ponderous and portentous, would be coaxed to start lighting the Tortoise stoves in school.

The shortening days had their own glories – the flaming berries were everywhere, their ripening no longer resented. Red haws crowded our hawthorn trees with chatter of feasting birds, vermilion hips hung like lanterns in the hedgerows; wreaths of woody nightshade berries dripped with gorgeous jewelled clusters of emerald, topaz and ruby ("don't pick them, they're poisonous"). Best of all perhaps was the enchanting pink and orange of the spindle which grew in some of the more distant hedges. A walk after school to find it would end in near darkness, with hands tingling cold, a red sunset behind the dark fir trees at the foot of the Hill, and frosty stars sharp in the pale sky. There might be potato cakes for tea when we got in, browned in the frying pan, spread with butter or dripping and eaten with salt – one of my mother's most tasty specialities, which I have tried in vain to reproduce since. Happy and replete, we would settle down to the rediscovered indoor pleasures of the longer evenings.

Susie's birthday fell at around this time, marked by the usual present-giving and another of my mother's memorable cakes. (I can just remember the stage when she was considered too young for anything but a plain sponge cake, but she soon broke the rich fruit cake barrier). The year's cycle in farm and garden was consummated by the Harvest Festival. Straightforward, glorious, down to earth, it held an immediacy for us, close to the land as we then were, which I miss in even village Harvest Festivals today. From the packed pews rang out all the old favourites, well known melodies lifting the heart in an hour's true praise; our eyes were feasted by the bunches of well-scrubbed carrots, beetroot and turnips, the apples in basket or paper-lined shoe-box, the two sheaves of corn at the chancel steps, Old Shep's best marrows taking pride of place. Many a side-long glance would be cast to check that one's own produce was visible, and was, quite

definitely was, superior to everyone else's. Dahlias and Michaelmas daisies completed the joyful riot of colour. "Hymns Ancient and Modern" used to include a special hymn "For Use In Times Of Poor Harvest" but I doubt if it was ever sung. Yet there was a tinge of sadness, a feeling of the dying of the year; once Harvest Festival was over, little time remained before the setting in of the winter, for all the glory of the golden October days.

Not that they were all golden. There would come days of wind and scudding grey cloud, when seagulls flew high over the village with plaintive, other-worldly cries, and the old folks looked up wisely and said "Storms at sea". These days infected me, once, with an odd restlessness, a yearning, for which I must borrow a phrase from C.S. Lewis. (That most generous of men, dear friend in my eyes though known only in his books, with whose imaginative childhood mine has more that a little in common, would surely allow it). In "Surprised By Joy" he recounts how one of the Beatrix Potter books, "Squirrel Nutkin", "troubled me... with the the Idea of Autumn." The grey windy days troubled me with the Idea of the Sea – why, I cannot tell. It was not the tamed, potted sea of Weston trips for which I longed, but wet sheets and flowing winds, crashing waves, a tall ship and a star to steer her by – the kind of essence of the Sea which was known to me only in books. It was an acute desire, short-lived, poignant, very real while it lasted, and inexplicable to me still.

Looking up at the Hangings, we watched the late summer green give way to a patchwork of gold, flame and bronze. The end of the playground was a-flutter with the fallen yellow leaves of the elm trees. Horse chestnuts were thwacked down from the great tree next to the pub garage by impatient boys who knew in their bones that it was conker time and could not wait for the autumn gales. No matter when we went out conkering, the boys always seemed to have been there already, leaving only the second best to reward our search among the golden brown, astringent-tanged fallen leaves. But any conker is a delight – polished, satiny, filling the hand with its cool satisfying knobbliness. It was the collecting we loved; we did not play seriously at "conkers", but just amassed, admired, swapped and handled them till old age robbed them of their sheen and hints of mould appeared. Even then, the soundest could be peeled and made excellent cottage loaves for the dolls' house inhabitants.

Best of all, perhaps, at this time of year, was the Beech Walk. You could climb up the Hill, follow the edge of a meadow on the top, and then find a steep diagonal path downwards across the slope of the Hangings, where the silver boles of ancient beech trees rose high into the sky, and their fallen leaves lay in deep drifts through which we ploughed, kicking them up into a whirling, swirling, copper-brown storm. As the meadow cranesbill was our flower of the summer, so was the beech our tree in the autumn. Down the steep slope we plunged, exposed tree-roots in the bare earth (for little will grow under the deep shade of beech trees) forming a natural staircase – then back across the fields, through the quiet friendly churchyard and home.

So, gently but inexorably, the year drew towards its close. Autumn ploughing was over, winter wheat sown. Cows were brought in at night. The land began its winter sleep, stillness masking the continued unseen growth. For us too there was a sense of marking time, a period without major events. Remembrance Day (Armistice Day, as it was then called, before it became the commemoration of two world wars) passed solemnly. The church bell tolled out the Two Minutes' Silence for which farm workers paused, heads bared, while in school the children, with poppies pinned to jerseys and jackets, stood manfully as still and silent as they could. What an endless two minutes it seemed, and how hard to focus one's thoughts as directed, in gratitude and remembrance. The bell tolled again. The school piano sounded the opening chords of the hymn "O God, our help in ages past". Awed and moved by the silence, united by who knows what stories of family loss, the whole school sang as one. Just as the quiet fields now lay preparing for next season's fruitfulness, so, we dimly sensed, the quiet dead whose names gleamed proudly on the village War Memorial in the church (where the Guides would lay a wreath of poppies on Sunday), mown down in the fields of Flanders, had brought forth fruits of peace and freedom for all time, or so for a few years still, we believed.

As if to cheer us, there might still come odd days when the sun shone hazily but warm, and our winter coats could be discarded for an hour or so. But they were fleeting and illusory, and we knew it. Enjoy them, but Winter is really our business now. And suddenly, with chill of fog and nip of frost, robins still singing solos of heartrending sweetness and lamps lit at four o'clock, the once unattainable "next Christmas" is within sight again. Carols are practised in school. The day is set for the Great Shopping Expedition. I have thought up a present for Susie, but what on earth can I give to Phil? We sit in corners in our spare time, trying to hide the purses or pen-wipers or whatever small objects we are making for each other. The joys of Christmas are in the air again. The cycle of our year is all but complete. And if you think, (and I would not disagree) that it has taken a long time to get us from one Christmas to the next – well, a year is a long time when you are four, five or even six.

I Must Write to Bumpus

I cannot remember either being unable to read, or the process of learning. I know that we all read at an early age, with the help first of letter blocks and then of a series of little books of unimaginable dullness – primers which today would be considered likely to put a child off reading for life, but had no such effect on us. Ned and Sam (I think) plodded their way through page after page of the "Ned is in bed. Sam has a cap" variety. One rather more spirited passage captivated us greatly. The venue was the top of a horse-drawn bus, whence Ned's (or Sam's) hat blew off. But succour was at hand –

"Oh, oh, my hat is off.

Get my hat.

The man will get my hat.

Thank you, man."

To this day, if one of us gives the cue, another will complete the well-worn lines, amidst peals of laughter, and we are four and five years old again.

From this foundation course I think we graduated to reading "real books" with help. I recall stumbling through pages of "Nature's Pageant", garnering titbits of information about frogspawn and celandines, stoats and squirrels, and adoring the bright glossy illustrations. Intransigent words were lightly ringed in pencil by my father. "We'll put a house round that one, so that you can remember it". The method certainly worked. We were soon reading fluently and avidly, the mechanics mastered, the sense trailing behind the sound. One final stage I do remember. Outside the back door in the sunshine with my book of the moment, I heard my father's voice call "Try to say the words inside your mind – you don't need to say them out loud when you are reading." I tried, and was astonished that it worked. A layer of our cocoon had split, and a new dimension of being was mine.

So, books and reading became early an indispensable part of our lives. Early, too, did my father establish himself as guardian of literary-moral standards. For years I don't think we ever opened a book which he had not previously vetted. At first there were annuals. Bobby Bear, Maisie Mouse and Ruby Rabbit delighted us all. Some lesser annual yielded the fairy stories of Agnes Grozier Herbertson – so enchanting, inspired, free of any taint of sickly-sweetness, that I am saddened and surprised to find how few people of our generation seem to know them. One, "The Spindle Tree", surviving in book form, is still a cherished possession of Susie's; her children in turn revelled in it, and we all re-read it with joy from time to time. Yumps the Gnome, the One-Shoe Dwarf, the Tip-Toe Common, the Spindle Tree herself, the exquisite little verses embroidered into the text – all of these will live as long as we do, and may the book hold together for Susie's grandchildren, when there are any.

My much loved "ABC of Birds" must have belonged to this early period. A picture and a verse for each letter of the alphabet – and if some of the verses erred a little on the arch side, I wasn't aware of it then.

"F stands for Flamingo –
What very thin legs!
He ought to knit stockings
To cover such pegs."

And Z was neatly side-stepped.

"Z stands for the Zoo
(You surely have been)
Where most of these birds
Can (for sixpence) be seen." Sixpence indeed......

But real books soon took over. They were a regular feature of Christmas, and sometimes appeared unexpectedly at other seasons as well. My father must have spent hours poring over reviews and publishers' catalogues throughout the year to keep up the supply. Early in the autumn we would hear him drop the magic words "I must write to Bumpus'". Then we rejoiced and hugged ourselves mentally, for we knew that the hunt was up. The letter would go – probably written by my mother in the end, as my father loathed the writing of letters. And in due course the parcels would begin to arrive – huge, weighty, tantalising – pounds and stones of future joy, encased in layers of stout brown paper and knotted around with hairy white string. They sat majestically in the empty Front Room

by day; and late into the night, while we slept above, my father read, judged, rejected, and approved. It was one of the highlights of his year too, I imagine, and he made the most of it. He would report progress, but mysteriously; authors and titles never passed his lips. Sometimes, as we grew older, we were allowed to read the better rejects, the almost-approved, before they were sent back, after great performances of hand-washing, don't-crease-the-pages and don't-bend-the-backs. This was heady excitement, for our appetite for something new to read was immense. Occasional rejects proved so absorbing that we secretly wished that they could have been kept, but it would have been emphatically "not done" in our family to say so. Eventually the final choice was made. The rejects were parcelled up again and sent on their way back to Oxford Street. The chosen lay hidden till Christmas Day, when each of us would receive a small pile of three or four, and there might also be a few to put "on the shelf" for communal ownership. Another year's certain pleasure lay ahead.

And certain it was. To a child of today, used to a plentiful supply of beautiful books in school and to choice in a Public Library, as well as, one hopes, personal ownership at home, we might seem in this (and other!) respects incomprehensible. But we were children of few possessions. Books were our most vital resources for wet days and long evenings, the basis and inspiration for endless fantasy games and colloquies. Read and re-read, our prime favourites became so much part of our mental furniture that phrases, sentences, whole paragraphs from them came welling up into our daily conversation. Some of them are with us still –

"Did I lose my tail on the willow tree?

Did I lose my tail on the willow tree?

My tail? Rabbit's tail," lamented an absent-minded rabbit supposed to have been the original source of pussy-willow.

When Phil murmurs the first line of this even today, and I complete it for her, we are not really mad; one of us has simply mislaid something, and as we search we are taking the opportunity to revisit our common literary heritage – one of our strongest bonds now that, inevitably, all three of us have followed diverging paths and destinies.

Pleasure from new books was certain, too, because we were on the whole biddable children, apt to like what we were expected to like and to extract every shred of enjoyment from our rare treats. Some of my father's choices were conventional enough. Past and emergent children's classics rubbed shoulders on our shelves – Anderson and Grimm, "The Wind in the Willows", "Alice in Wonderland", "Black Beauty", "Treasure Island", "Little Women" and (gradually) its sequels. Some of his omissions were remarkable; why, for example, did we never meet Beatrix Potter? The "Dr Dolittle" books, then new, came our way, and the zany Professor Branestawm with vintage Heath Robinson illustrations convulsed us. But there were odd choices too. My father dated all books as they were bought, so that I can now look back and wonder what I can possibly have made, say, of Edmund Gosse's "Father and Son" at the age of eleven. So ravenous were our literary appetites, however, that everything was read, and only the frequency of re-reading and quoting would betray our preferences.

There was poetry too for the devouring, and favourite lines embedded themselves like nuggets of gold in the memory, to be taken out and savoured at intervals, and to feed our insatiable appetites for words, words, and more words.

New books heralded a collective pleasure too. In the dark lamplit evenings after Christmas, family tradition had it that my mother read aloud, one after another, most if not all of the new books. And what a reader she was! Clustered round the table, elbows propping small chins, my father relaxed in his armchair, we were immobilised, spellbound. The evening ticked away. The lamp burned low and was supplemented by a candle. The night chill of the draughty old house gently turned our feet to ice. We neither knew nor cared. We were merciless, pleading for "one more chapter" till my mother was often hoarse. Eventually some one would realise the time. "Those girls MUST go to bed". The book closes, my mother is complimented on her reading. We stretch, rub eyes that are tight with concentration. Dizzy with the ecstasies of our latest new world, we drink our cocoa, climb the dark stairs and are tucked into bed. As our feet slowly thaw, sleep claims us one by one, and we fall into dreams coloured by the wonders of the evening, imaginations fed and fuelled ready for the next day.

Summer bedtimes held bookish pleasures of another kind. My mother was as gifted a raconteuse as reader. The traditional fairy stories came first, pruned of any frightening elements. Later there were tales of her own early life, which we loved, and requested over and over again. "Tell us that one about when you all had measles together… about the midnight feasts at College… about when you were in Egypt…" She recalled and re-told, too, favourite books from her childhood – "Little Men", "Huckleberry Finn", (which we thought hilariously funny – the underlying tragedy only came home to us much later), to mention just two which we first met in this way. Safe in bed, we revelled in every word, begging for "a little bit more" to prolong both the magic and the bright day, which the Grown-Ups terminated so arbitrarily for us with the inexorable call of "bedtime".

As we grew older, my father must have relaxed his censorship slightly, to admit the harmless as well as the first-rate. Those were the days when the village school was often the local depot of the County Library, and Heads took the issuing of books as a normal extra duty, (unpaid, of course). The stock was changed two or three times a year – another great event. Gradually, library books began to be tolerated, though still vetted, and handed over with a grudging "Well, I suppose it can't do you any harm". Only the less battered volumes were permissible, and hands must be washed after reading them, as you never know where they have been. They filled a need, and I don't think they permanently lowered our literary tastes. Through them we practised a kind of escapism, enjoyed experiences which our way of life denied. I devoured Angela Brazil and Gunby Hadath (did ever any writer invent so many ways of avoiding the word "said"? His characters breathed, mouthed, hissed, gurgled, but never did they say anything). I revelled in the "Biggles" books, in tales of Brownies and Guides performing incredible "good turns". The mildest of adult novels were by degrees allowed, but we must have been well into our teens before my father's benevolent censorship ended.

At some stage the magazine of the Girl Guide Movement received the "All Clear" and became a weekly pleasure. Unwaveringly high-principled, it was full of good things – short stories and serials, woodcraft, hints on obtaining badges, letters for and from the handicapped, accounts of Guide events at home and abroad. And I shall always feel affection for the "Farmer's Weekly", which must have pertained to the rural subjects taught valiantly by my mother in school. It was not only the pages specially for the farmer's wife and children that we enjoyed; we also gleaned fascinating snippets of information on milk yields, pig-rearing, root crops and poultry-keeping. Phil's passion for Jersey cows was sustained by articles and pictures. The advertisements were fascinating too – who now remembers Dr. Burdizzo's Bloodless Castrator, or Millie the Million Gallon Cow?

On yet another plane was my mother's "Good Needle-work" magazine, which I remember as largely devoted to embroidery, with occasional free transfer patterns thrown in. We gasped at the apparently limitless possibilities – firescreens of Anne Hathaway's cottage, a design of horse-chestnut leaves in beautiful cut-work on a tray-cloth, cushions in petit point and tapestry work. No doubt my mother's skilful fingers itched for the time and money to try them all. As for us three, Phil developed a love of cross-stitch, my sticky needle achieved the odd lazy-daisy, and Susie, as usual, bided her time. But there was an illicit thrill. The needlework content was laced with the lightest and most improbable romances, and the pages of these were supposed to be stuck together before we saw the magazine. Sometimes a paragraph or two, set in the middle of instructions for A Tea Cosy In Satin Stitch, or Making A Beautiful Afternoon Tea Cloth, would prove impossible to conceal. We were trusted in such a case not to read, and I did my best, but my memories of appliqué and feather stitch still carry a whiff of the Far East – She Married a Sheikh, and that kind of thing.

When all other supplies failed, we would pester my father for "a book from the Front Room" or "something out of your

Box Upstairs". For the Front Room held the family stock of "grown-up books", and the Box Upstairs, a collection from my father's student days. A row of volumes of "The World's Best Short Stories" yielded (by permission) the occasional gem, and from the Box descended, gradually, old Everyman editions of the classics – Scott, Dickens, Thackeray, Jane Austen, George Eliot – some of which we grew to love. I ploughed doggedly, word by word, through Scott; I never really enjoyed "Old Mortality", blood and torture being little to my taste, but parts of "Ivanhoe" were exciting, and anyway, it was something to read. Only one book do I wish that I had been forbidden – Harrison Ainsworth's "Old St. Paul's". Its graphic accounts of the Plague and the Fire of London filled me with real horror and haunted me for weeks. Every innocent passing manure cart was transformed by my too active imagination into a plague cart full of suppurating corpses, and not for anything would I re-read it even now.

If desperate, I would sit by the hour over the bound volumes of the "Children's Dictionary". I can see them now – faded red spines with gold lettering proclaiming the contents as Harken to Male (my father would quote this, in humorous vein, to reinforce instructions, which struck us as exquisitely funny), Male to Polder, Snail to Zymotic. The illustrations were copious and the colour plates a particular joy. (No matter if they did lead me to visualize the kingfisher as the size of a jackdaw). I collected facts and meanings to hoard like that same jackdaw, and perhaps best of all, began to know something of the derivations and histories of words – an interest which I still regard as one of my father's best legacies. We were a dictionary-minded family in any case; mealtime conversation tended to be punctuated by "Get the Oxford Dictionary" or the bird book, or the wild flower book, or even the Encyclopedia Britannica, which sat smugly in its own bookcase in the Front Room. In later childhood I tried hard, and furtively, to inform myself from it on subjects not touched on elsewhere. But pore as I would over Obstetrics or Prostitution, even the E.B. never told me quite what I wanted to know…

So we read our way through childhood, informed, enriched, entertained, finally to achieve independent judgement, never to lose our love of words and books.

As a postscript I cannot resist sketching the later stages of my father's contact with Bumpus. The time came, of course, when he stopped buying books for us; but he continued to "write to Bumpus", for many years, searching with growing difficulty for books to satisfy almost impossible literary standards of his own. It saddened me that he, to whom books had been one of the greatest pleasures of life, came to reject more and more as unworthy of his notice, and was left in his last years with only a handful which he could really enjoy. He became increasingly pre-occupied, too, with the bodies of his books, so that a flaw in the paper of one page would cause him to send the book back with a request for "a perfect copy". I recall a book once arriving in response with a note from the long-suffering Bumpus saying "This is *the most perfect copy* which the publishers can supply". He must have been a trying customer, perhaps even something of a legend at 477, Oxford Street. But when during his last illness he wrote for some unusual book, saying that he was gravely ill and wanted to read it before he died, he received a warm personal letter "to an old and valued customer" – followed very shortly, and in time, by the book.

No Friend like a Sister

I sometimes tried to imagine what it would have been like to be part of a family constellation different from the one in which I grew up, or to occupy a different position in it. Even my fertile imagination could not get very far with this. I could toy agreeably with notions of baby brothers, or speculate as to the possible pleasures of being a twin, but I always came back to the inarticulate but definitely felt conclusion that the me-ness of me was inextricably bound up with being just where I was in this particular family – two and a half years younger than Phil and a jealously guarded fifteen months older than Susie.

These family positions were of course a *fait accompli* to me, which may have accentuated the feeling – Phil being well established long before I arrived and Susie pre-dating the dawn of conscious memory. (I have a deep respect for the unconscious, but we will not, if you please, tangle with it here). I would not agree with those psychologists who see the position of the "middle child" as an especially perilous one, for I think each family position has its hazards and its advantages. Eldest children may benefit from their parents' undivided attention, but they may also find it a smothering affair. They suffer a good deal of trial and error and uncertain handling; are often required to act as pacemakers and example-setters; and in adolescence may have to blaze costly trails of independence. But their status is secure – once the eldest, always the eldest, however many times they have to adjust to further arrivals. A youngest child who remains, as Susie did, the youngest, also has an obvious status. Her lot will be some blend of petting and bullying from her older brethren, an upbringing in which they play a considerable part. She will be lucky if she does not suffer from comparisons, from urges both external and personal to grow up and achieve just a little faster than she really can; or, in contrast, there may be pressures to remain a baby. I have never envied either eldest or youngest children. As for my own middle position, it has a certain ambiguity of status, to be sure; as Winston Churchill is reputed to have said, when welcoming one Mr. Bossom to the House of Commons, it is neither one thing nor t'other. It may be true that "middles" have a tendency to self-assertiveness in consequence. But we also have our advantages. Our parents no longer bath a baby as if handling Dresden china, nor do they rush out to the pram every ten minutes to see if one is still breathing. We cannot enjoy, but we also do not have to endure, their undivided attention. Even if, in my case, the pace set by Phil was a pretty exacting one, the two and a half years' age gap saved me from overmuch pressure, while the very existence of Susie gave me some sense of the superiority of age. On the whole, I am well content to be a "middle", and the middle of a trio of sisters. One has to miss out on some experiences, such as being part of a mixed-sex family, or being fully aware of new arrivals. I am long past the point of envy; I am sure that these are precious (and perilous) experiences, but they would have produced a different "me", and that is just as unthinkable today as it was fifty years ago.

So my two sisters were essential to me, as no doubt I was to them. That is to say, in retrospect, for in childhood, it is usually only at moments of extreme frustration that one analyses one's relationships. When Phil and Susie played at "worriting Alison" I actively wished them a lot further. And when, after some particularly fierce quarrel, we had Christina Rossetti's "Goblin Market" (a slim limp-covered book "on the shelf") quoted at us –

"For there is no friend like a sister
In calm or stormy weather",

I am sure we all felt it was an over-rated sentiment. But normally we accepted each other, as we accepted ourselves, unquestioningly, and our daily shared experiences of living, growing, playing and reading became a deep communal store at the heart of our three personalities. Our recollections differ now in detail and emphasis, and some, vivid to one, are lost to the others; but the essentials are there, and with them the assurance of continuity with those inextinguishable childhood selves in the stone-built School House and the ever-sunny garden.

How do these small selves look, when I turn back the pages of my photograph album? All three are straight-haired, the short-cut style alternating between partings and fringes (and what heart-searchings there were, I well remember, each time the style was changed); Phil and Susie sturdy, myself on the skinny side, with the round glasses I wore from the age of five as inevitable a part of me as nose or ears. Phil is fair, serious in many of the photographs; I start fair and turn mousy; and Susie, captured by the camera at exactly the stage at which I first recall her, is a round scrap with wispy dark hair. As we grow older the pictures show an inherent family resemblance among us, alongside definite individualities of feature, expression and stance. Susie loses her wispiness and becomes the best-looking. We appear sometimes singly but more often in trio – on the sands at Weston; sitting in the massively heavy wooden wheelbarrow in the garden; surrounded by dolls at a "dolls' tea-party"; as Brownies, as Guides, with cats, among chickens; and every photograph is vibrant with the memory of relationship as well as event and setting.

Phil's seniority could not be denied. She was always taller than me; she was admitted earlier into some of the Grown-Ups' councils, could write beautifully when I was still struggling, and seemed to have amazing skill with a needle and at the piano before I touched either. She did different lessons both in school and at home, mysteriously knew and understood things I didn't, read harder books, incurred household chores sooner and oftener than I. Occasionally her status was marked by some treat for which Susie and I were considered too young, and which she would describe to us minutely afterwards, while we listened with a mixture of awe and envy, sure that we would not have been too young to appreciate it. Thus she witnessed the christening of a friend's baby (we were all reproved for playing at christening our dolls afterwards – it was "not the right sort of thing to play at", we were told). She was taken to Swindon for a few swimming lessons; and at one time had sixpence a week pocket money, while Susie and I had only a penny. (Equality was restored when all our pocket money vanished as the depression of the 1930's bit harder and deeper). Phil was always in charge on our expeditions to fetch the milk. Susie or I might carry the empty can down to the farm, but she felt it her duty to carry the full one back. She took her responsibilities seriously, and rarely, if ever, did she lead us in any way astray. Lead she undoubtedly did – whence some quarrels and fights with me in particular were inevitable. The distinction between leadership and "bossiness" is always a pretty blurred one, and while I admired Phil's superior attainments I was very touchy about being bossed.

I was touchy too, I'm afraid, as I grew older, about anything which seemed to threaten my precious fifteen months' seniority over Susie. I was used to the collective "the girls" for the three of us, but I much disliked being classed with Susie as "the little ones". There was a long period when we were all dressed alike. We didn't particularly care for this, but when Phil was allowed different styles of a more Grown-Up nature, and Susie and I remained at a lower level together, I actively disliked it, though I never said so. Worse still, Susie gradually equalled my height, and I was infuriated for several years by people who asked if we were twins – it seemed a real threat to my identity. (Quite different, of course, from those fantasies of a twinhood which I would somehow have chosen). And Susie would no more be bossed by me than I by Phil – so there would be verbal fights, pushes that turned to slaps, tears and reproaches. I look back on this aspect of learning to live with a smile of compassion for three sturdy young personalities, thrown perhaps too closely together by our near-isolation as a family, thrusting their sometimes troubled way onwards from a basis of so much shared lore and experience that the quarrels now seem mere ripples on the surface of deep water.

Some of them, indeed, really were very funny. Susie at the round and wispy stage was nobody's fool. She knew well enough that Phil and I were expected to cherish her tenderly and that Grown-Up wrath would follow swiftly on any suspicion of unkindness on our part. During the early morning period when we were supposed to amuse ourselves quietly till it was time to get up, she might disappear silently underneath the bedclothes – an ominous signal which Phil and I knew only too well. What was the matter, we would ask, leaning dangerously out of our adjoining beds, or even, forbidden though it was, climbing out of them to hang solicitously over her cot. "I am offended" would come a muffled voice. What had we done? "Plenty" was the inevitable and only response; and there would follow coaxings, pettings, promises of rare treats like colouring in a page of Phil's best crayoning book (she really hated to have it marred by the smudgy efforts of us smaller fry), or choosing what we should play all day, before the little puss gradually emerged from the depths, red-faced and pink-eared (her ears stuck out and were known as "Susie's bath-handles") from warmth and suppressed – tears? or laughter? We never really knew which, but we counted ourselves lucky if she had been cajoled back to her usual sunny self before the Grown-Ups were around. No doubt she needed an occasional exercise of power, and I am sure she enjoyed it.

Waking hours in bed were always a challenge, especially at night. Small children who go to bed early, and whose pleas for one more story, one more episode of "when you were a little girl" or one last drink of water, are eventually refused, have to use up their still abundant energy somehow before they fall asleep. Anything violent, like bouncing on one's bed forcefully enough to send it jogging across the room, was too audible to be worth more than a very occasional try. An exciting game invented by Phil, of diving head first down under the bedclothes and scrabbling one's way out at the bottom of the bed, was also actively discouraged. I hated it anyway, and only played it to keep my end up with Phil – I who can still experience panic if trapped by a stuck zip with a dress over my head, floundered frantically in the dark stuffy depths, and never expected to come out alive. Pulling loose bits of wallpaper off the damp bedroom walls was tempting, but led to trouble. Yet another lovely game had a disastrous conclusion. Each of us had a "special" blanket with a border of many colours, and we found it a delightful occupation to pick off bits of coloured fluff and sort them neatly into piles of pink, blue, yellow or green. As I worked away quietly but enthusiastically one light evening, nothing was further from my thoughts than making a hole in the blanket. I was horrified when one appeared, and the permanent presence of a darn in my beautiful blanket was quite sufficient punishment to me and warning to the other two. (Less mild was my fate when I deliberately, but in a spirit of scientific enquiry, used the scissors to cut a small hole in the front of my dark blue pinafore edged with red binding. My explanation, that I wanted to see what would happen, seemed a lame one as soon as it passed my lips…)

By degrees elaborate verbal games evolved in bed. They were much safer, as long as voices were kept reasonably low, and when indulged in at night could be terminated by the sleepy at will. Over a period of some years they developed into well understood systems with their own peculiar brand of logic. The whole thing began, as far as I can remember, with someone's discovery of the useful space created by sitting up in bed with knees drawn up and pointed outwards at an angle. This produced a handy dip in the bedclothes, oddly named a "woe". It could be used practically to accommodate small toys;

but being an interesting personal kind of space the "woe" soon gained some imaginative status. Anything captured (in imagination) from another and placed (in imagination) in one's "woe" was forfeit. Rapidly, the "woe" developed almost magical qualities, became a place where the will of the owner reigned supreme and where others entered by permission only. As the imaginative concept widened, the visible dip in the bed-clothes lost its importance. The "woe" was succeeded by the "Dolland" (one word, but with some obvious etymological connections with "doll-land"), and it was in our Dollands that we disported ourselves in fluent imaginative interchange, night after night for some years.

Children are very much at the mercy of even the best of Grown-Ups, and to have an area, if only an imagined one, where the child is in charge, must have great relief value. I am sure that our Dollands had this useful function, as well as being enormous fun. The rulers – Miss Phil, Miss Alison and Miss Susie (shades here of "Cranford", which we read and loved from an early age) – arranged internal affairs to suit themselves, mapped them out in lengthy soliloquies, invited their counterparts to visit, strictly on their own terms, and entertained them with minutely described festivities and grave discussions on matters of state. Phil, typically, organised her Dolland to the nth degree, even inventing a language for it and writing her own grammar; Susie was an apt pupil, but I was resistant, and when traces of Phil's language began to mingle with Susie's embryonic French exercises, it was firmly discouraged. Miss Phil had children, I think, though no obvious husband that I can recall. Miss Alison had an enormous brood of children (who were also drawn on large sheets of cardboard, coloured with crayons and cut out), all with interesting and differing personalities. There were twins, Mabel and Agnes – one naughty and one almost saintly;

Alfred was the bad boy, Little Jim a rather wet character, Joan an engaging two-year-old. Muriel, Violet and I don't know how many others of lesser personality also figured in the family. But in my Dolland the sexes lived in separate halves of the country, boys being removed at the age of seven, and husbands visiting their wives only occasionally – I had a vague idea that this was somehow necessary for the continuation of the species. It was an arrangement made, I imagine, in pique after some minor brush with my father, and once set up, was impossible to reverse. It made life in my Dolland simpler, anyway... The details of Susie's Dolland escape my memory, but she was well able to keep her end up in the spirited exchanges involved.

One of the conventions was that when you had said something, it was so, in your own Dolland, for ever and ever, and exclusively. Occasional latent elements of spite could thus be worked off, verbally of course, in the lengthy conversations of the game. There was a floating character known as "the-man-who-comes-to-see-the-inside-of-your-house-to-see-if-it's-all-tidy". If one could be verbally agile enough to "plant" him in one of the other domains, and to get in first by describing the chaos he found, in, say, Miss Phil's house (before she leapt in to describe its perfect order), this was a deadly insult, perhaps a sweet piece of revenge. (I have known other small children really distressed by threats to "draw a picture of you in a horrible frock" or to "draw you without your knickers on". Both the spoken word and the drawing have some almost magical significance). One of the three rulers, I forget which, was landed with the reputation of only visiting the others on their "grocery day", i.e. the day when the mythical shop had delivered the mythical supplies which, like our real ones, might be a little thin by the end of the week. And was there a little spite in the exchange that rose to poetic heights as follows, or was it all good clean fun?

Miss Phyllis decided to visit her friend
Miss Susie, so well known.
So to her house she then did wend –
She set out all alone.

She found Miss Susie in her bed
Crying into a hutch.
Her favourite guinea pig was dead!
"I do not weep for such,

And don't think I e'er care one bit"
Said Phil, that horrid freak
Which was a fib – she'd had a fit,
When her pet died, and cried for a week.

Poetic imagination tailed off here; I remember being told by
my mother, to whom we unwisely recited our effort, that it
wasn't very nice to call one's sister a horrid freak "even in a
poem", but I really believe that our chief aim that time had
been to find a rhyme for "week". In the main, Dollands were
amiable and vastly enjoyable. If you think it all very odd, read
C.S. Lewis's "Surprised by Joy", or Eiluned Lewis's lovely

"Dew on the Grass", and see how other imaginative children have played similar games; if odd, we were in very good company.

Often, when the affairs of our Dollands had been satisfactorily settled, and contented deep breathing came from Phil's and Susie's beds, I would be still wide awake and lively. I was the odd poor sleeper sandwiched in between two good ones. I remember a phase when, having read or heard of someone who died in her sleep, I deliberately kept awake in case the same thing should happen to me, but I don't think this accounted for my continual wakefulness. It was all terribly boring. I could call for drinks of water a couple of times without waking the other two (which would have been a crime). I could creep downstairs, pathetically, to say I couldn't sleep and to see what the Grown-Ups were doing. It never seemed very interesting, but I might be given some thing to eat – bread-and-butter with sugar, or a handful of sultanas – or allowed to stay for a few minutes, snuggled into my mother's lap while she ploughed on with the day's pile of Arithmetic or English Composition books. Then back up to bed, and with luck, to sleep. If this did not work, there were two possible mitigators of wakefulness which I loved. My mother might place a candlestick, holding the dying end of a lit candle, in the top of the green china jug which stood on our old-fashioned, marble-slabbed washstand. I would lie entranced, watching the flame leap and fall and cast changing shadows on to the sloping ceiling, and often my eyes would close before the glowing candle wick gave a last flare and flickered into extinction. The other treat was the loan of a precious shawl of my mother's, dating from her party-going and dancing days as a young girl, when, she told me, it would have been called a "fascinator". It was made of creamy-coloured silk with a knitted texture, and had traces of blue, pink and gold in the border; best of all, it had a deep fringe, the silken heaviness of which I can still feel in my fingers. To hold and handle this lovely thing was a dreamy joy, which again, often relaxed me into sleep. I wonder what eventually became of that shawl? But the infallible remedy was to hear the sounds of the Grown-Ups downstairs ending their long day. My mother was always the last, and the gentle click of the door at the bottom of the stairs, followed by her quiet ascent (but some of the stairs creaked, on exactly the right note of reassurance) acted like a charm. Many times I have heard the door click, and then been asleep before she reached the top of the stairs to look, shaded candle in hand, into "the girls' room", and no doubt sigh with relief that sleep had claimed me at last.

I don't remember feeling any the worse for these wakeful nights. They certainly did not diminish my appetite for living by day. Surely, the whole-heartedness of childhood must be the stuff of which the Kingdom of Heaven is made, rather than simplicity or teachableness, as some would have it. Phil, Susie and I daily awoke full of eager anticipation of the joys of another day. We were right up to the neck in everything we did, and nearly all of our interests were shared interests, our pursuits communal ones, our imaginative games dependent on three participants. Not always, of course. There were times when Phil and Susie appeared to exclude me – often, I am sure, due to my own obstinate fault. Phil and I had phases of superiority to Susie, whispering in corners things we thought her too young to understand. Susie and I, when the weight of "lessons" had descended more heavily on Phil, were much in each others' company. But my essential recollections are of the long hours spent all three together – playing endlessly with balls in the school playground (where Susie infuriated me by mastering "two balls" before I did), or swooping over the hard surface on our scooters. Or balancing, arms outspread, along the edge of the low vertical board which separated the asphalt section of the playground from the rough grass, and which we called the kerb. You could cover its length easily without slipping off if someone walked beside supporting you, but to do it alone was quite a feat. For reasons now unknown to me, when playing this game we were Peggy, Poggy and Piggy. "Round, Peggy!" we would call to our support, if wanting to turn and make a return journey, or "Out of my way, Poggy!" if two of us approached from opposite ends and one had to give way – you could not pass without falling off. We grubbed in our gardens, for we had a little plot each; and played elaborate games with our dolls. They were as nearly live people to us as they could be, though on their own plane and never quite equated with reality. They had to be fed, and as realistically as possible; so the dry brown seeds of dock plants were stripped from their stems for dolls' coffee, red-tinged stones were admirable dolls' meat, the short thick stalks of the broad-leafed burr which grew in a corner of the playground served as dolls' rhubarb, and dandelion leaves made good dolls' lettuce. Phil of the clever fingers actually made a miniature mincing machine for dealing with dolls' food, from cocoa tins cut up with the kitchen scissors; even though it would only mince up the dandelion leaves, it was an impressive achievement. The dolls had a continual need for new clothes, too, and all my mother's skill and patience was at our disposal to help us with sewing or knitting them; as we grew older, Phil became almost equally skilled, and even I would accept her guidance respectfully if my mother was not available.

Reading was shared too – and what we read was soon translated into our play, so that a Robin Hood phase would be succeeded by "Knights of the Round Table" with cardboard armour, and a fright for me when Phil stabbed me with a sword previously dipped in red paint. We planned for Susie to keep vigil over her armour in a dark passage for an hour, prior to her knighting ceremony, and were a little annoyed when my mother made us reduce the time to five minutes. She was right, of course, but I think we felt that our play plans were one part of our lives where Grown-Ups ought not to intervene unless invited.

A rather curious game was the herding of cows (marbles) on carefully defined areas of the living-room carpet. It had been a good one in its day (several generations back in my mother's family), Persian I think, and had still, in the least worn areas, angular markings quite useful as field boundaries. Twelve inch rulers kept the cows from straying, and there were even songs (of a kind) specially composed for calling in the herds.

"Come in, dear cow
I want you now"
is admittedly not brilliant, nor is
"Come in, dear calf
We will not laugh",
but there is a ring of originality at least in
"Come in, dear heifer,
I think you will be seifer
With me than the wolf"
and
"Come in, dear bull,
You shall always eat your full".

Then there was the game of "patterns". These were the little books of material samples which my mother used when ordering her school needlework supplies; some of them were non-returnable, and in due course came to us, to be carefully prised apart, examined, exclaimed over, and eventually shared out by the process of choosing in turn. Much heart-searching here – to choose that lovely scrap of pink flowered voile, but risk thereby losing the chance of a piece of bright red repp? Was either big enough to make something for one of the beautifully made three-inch-high china dolls which Woolworths produced at that time (alas, where are they now?), and which we dressed and re-dressed with real ingenuity? Heavier, plainer bits of tweed and the like tended to be chosen last, useful though we knew they would prove when Christmas approached and the inevitable pen-wipers were to be made. "Patterns" gave us hours of pleasure in sorting, arranging, re-arranging, swapping (but this last led to regrets, recriminations and squabbles, so was discouraged). One piece of a sort of episcopal purple shade, with a silky texture, I recall as seeming to all of us the ultimate in desirability. Phil had acquired it, legitimately, but Susie and I yearned dreadfully for it. It was several years later that Phil, turning out her oddments box, re-discovered it and gave it to me quite casually, as a thing of little worth. I was dumbfounded at her generosity – maybe, without my realising it, she was putting away childish things.

I had almost forgotten our "oddments boxes". Storage of our possessions, few though they were, must have been a problem in that small house. Dolls and soft toys, their ownership crystal-clear, lived happily enough in the outgrown baby cot. Books stayed firmly on their shelves except when actually being read – to leave one on the floor was considered a serious misdemeanour. (When in my teens I read a biography of Louisa May Alcott, I was quite shocked to learn that in her family books had been so plentiful as to be used for building houses and castles!) Phil had a desk, in which she kept her "good" paintbox and colouring books, her kaleidoscope and a few other treasures. But for small miscellaneous property there were three stout boxes; no doubt they had started life with our groceries in them. These were the "oddments boxes", kept in the cupboard-under-the-stairs (along with brown paper, scooters, and a supposedly fly-proof meat-safe), each absolutely sacred to its owner. We would not have dreamed of looking in anyone else's oddments box – an understanding which must have forestalled many arguments. You might find in mine, as well as marbles and "patterns", a ruler, a scruffy paintbox, a couple of damaged small toys which I couldn't bear to throw away, a half-finished piece of "embroidery" in which I had lost interest, a bag of special stones, some rather gritty crayons, a collection of scrap paper for drawing on, a few motheaten dolls' clothes, an exercise book containing my current literary work, and Heaven only knows what else. All safe from marauding hands, though we would enjoy turning out and comparing the contents of our boxes quite frequently together.

Together we watched Miss Bridgeman's chickens, together we dogged her footsteps as much as we could when she came to feed the birds, clean out the chicken-houses or collect the eggs. Together we gathered worm-casts and modelled ducks (easy) and birds' nests from the soft malleable stuff; melted down candle-ends in shoe-polish tins to provide a different modelling material (but after a tin of melted wax had capsized on the carpet this game had an abrupt end).

Together we "talked" our favourite books, a pursuit we can still enjoy today. Together, together, together! Happy hours and days indeed, never long enough, when all life lay ahead and the store of shared experience was a-building, permeated always by the blessed, earth-based, seasonal background which grew deep into our very souls.

Yet, without contradiction, I can aver that we were always three distinct and disparate personalities. As we became older, so did some of our interests diverge, or shared activities were carried out at more obviously differing levels. When we all developed a passion for fretwork (and I blush now to think of some of the floridly designed articles which we perpetrated) it was Phil the persevering who planned and produced a beautiful scale replica of Miss Bridgeman's henhouse. It was Phil the reverently compassionate animal- and bird-lover who stopped us from killing wasps, who handled great black slugs fearlessly and could see the beauty of all creation in them. How she must have suffered, really suffered, from the very small Susie's favourite game of stamping on luckless worms, then looking up with an angelic smile to announce with satisfaction "I've deaded it". But a slightly older Susie loved earwigs and woodlice, even kissing them – we always dreaded that she would swallow one by mistake – and adoringly patted "dear little kidneys" floured ready for frying. As for me, I rejoiced in almost any living creature (large house-spiders only excepted), but without the whole-hearted devotion which, focussed particularly on birds, gave Phil the status of family ornithologist.

Phil acquired a further, most enviable status as a sort of by-product of her "swimming trips" to Swindon. In a shop window she saw a large doll, real baby size, with china head, fair hair, blue eyes that opened and shut, and dimpled limbs made of "competition" – Susie's accepted misnomer for the "composition" of which her large, battered boy doll John Willie (green knitted suit and a somewhat raffish nature) was said to be made. Apparently Phil was deeply smitten by this lovely object, costing the (then) huge sum of twelve-and-six, and mortgaged her weekly sixpence for the next half-year in order to have it. (I believe the last few payments were benevolently cancelled in the end, but I am not sure of the details). So Pearl arrived – and in our eyes she was wholly beautiful, adorable and precious. That Phil should actually own anything so expensive and so exquisite! That she should occasionally, as a great favour, allow Susie and me to hold her, or to assist in undressing and re-dressing her in her wardrobe of the best of our disused baby-clothes! In truth, this was about all that one could do with Pearl, for she was too big as well as too other-worldly to play with. She could never, for instance, have been fitted into the old wooden dolls' pram which we bumped over the stony patch outside the back door, and out of which my precious Josephine bounced one terrible day, splitting her china skull in two. Josephine! Beloved even when scarred by this catastrophe, dressed as a "long-clothes baby" in the mode of yesteryear with knitted body-belt, flannel "barracot", pin-tucked and lace-trimmed gown, all laboriously made by me under my mother's instruction – even Josephine could not hold a candle to Pearl. Nor could my much smaller Lucy, for all the splendour of the pink-and-blue organdie outfit in which she arrived one Christmas; nor Olive, dark haired, sultry and mysterious; nor Barbara, in a blue one-piece sleeping suit. As for Andrew – but Andrew was a disappointment from the start, for in his white smock over short red trousers he fell far short of the vision of manliness I had in my mind when I asked for "a boy doll" for Christmas. Little squashy Winnie, whom you have already met as the awakener of an independent conscience in me, was nowhere in the race. Other, homemade, dolls, cut from the better pieces of discarded stockinette vests and stuffed with thistledown, or made out of old stockings, (like Alec, a deplorable character whom Susie and I tried hard, but unsuccessfully, to grind to powder in the treadle wheel of the sewing machine) – they faded into insignificance, they were less than dust, almost an insult to dollhood, in comparison with Pearl. When I acquired the purple "pattern", I kept a piece of Pearl's blonde hair given by Phil carefully wrapped in it for a considerable time, thus bringing together two rare and prized treasures. It is perhaps a sad reflection that possession can give status so early in life; yet there was something innocent and selfless in Phil's pride in her Pearl, her renunciation of her income for such an immensely long period.

Susie made her mark at an early age, with music. My mother, who came from a musically-talented family, was a capable pianist and organist, and could coax melody from violin, and later, 'cello too. Susie was the chief inheritor of this gift; she would creep into the front room and pick out tunes, one-fingered, on the piano long before her music lessons began, with my mother as teacher. When they did, she and I were taught, as often, together – an arrangement usually rather hard on Susie, for fifteen months can make quite a difference in the early stages of learning, say, French or Arithmetic. But with music our positions were reversed. I trailed behind Susie, my fingers stiff and disobedient where hers were nimble, my lot in the duets we practised always the easier part. I am sure this was good for both of us. I envied, rather than resented, Susie's undeniable skill as a performer, and long ago realized with deep gratitude that performance and appreciation are separable. Music – my kind of music – has been one of the abiding joys of my life, in no way marred by the recollection of the highest compliment my father ever paid to my piano-playing – "I thought it must have been Susie".

Between Phil the ornithologist and Susie the musician, where did I stand? As I have said, this kind of uncertainty can make us "middles" a bit uppish. My fatal propensity for "showing-off" – speaking when I should have been silent, or saying the wrong thing confidently – may well have been a reaction to middlehood. Once, I remember, when a visitor called, Susie and I were on the floor counting and re-counting our worldly wealth (mine was kept in a little green crocheted purse). Susie was quiet, as ever, but I eagerly told the visitor that I had five pennies and soon would have six, "and then I can change them for a silver sixpence". The kindly visitor at once opened her bag to look for a penny, but was restrained by my father; and I was reproved later for "hinting", though I actually had spoken in complete innocence. Another time, peering out of the window of the train on the way to Weston, I remarked far too loudly "What a very porterish porter I can see over there". Again I was hushed, but not before I had tasted flattery in the amused faces of other people. I should always behave very quietly in public places like railway carriages, I was told afterwards. "You don't want to be drawing other people's attention to yourself" – well, it was obvious that I was *supposed* not to want to. It had seemed all very innocent to me, but Grown-Ups are so unpredictable...... I was vaguely aware of a need for status. I read voraciously and was dubbed the family bookworm, but I am not sure that I really was more of a reader than Phil or Susie. I did develop, quite early, an interest in cooking, which my mother encouraged as far as the oilstove would allow, and which, like reading, has been a sustained one. I remember thinking that this was something, at any rate, by which to identify myself, though it hardly seemed as definite or indeed as respectable as ornithology or music.

It was only for the eyes of others that I needed a badge of identification, something to prevent me from being lost among "the girls" or "the little ones". Personally, I needed no convincing of my own uniqueness – I simply knew it, although my ponderings among the gooseberry bushes had failed to explain it. (Emily, in "A High Wind in Jamaica", took the same problem up to her refuge, the masthead, and also failed to solve it). I was a world unto myself, within myself. But separateness can be enhanced by togetherness. I was never more myself, in those early golden days, than when absorbed in some elaborate, earthy or imaginative game with my sisters. Two fair heads and one dark one cluster together, three pairs of grey eyes are alight with the joy of living. We may be talking eagerly, with laughter, or conversing gravely; we may, in the absorption of our chosen pursuit, have no use for words, because that which we have shared since before we can remember goes above and beyond overt communication. I can put my finger unerringly on Phil's and Susie's weak spots as they can on mine, but we can also tap each others' strengths. We speak the same language, stem from the same roots. Perhaps that is what Christina Rossetti was really talking about.

Going to Fetch the Milk

"Time for the milk, girls!"

Called down the stairs would come this signal from my father during the years when "going to fetch the milk" was a daily event of central importance in our lives. I have already hinted at its significance, and it is time now for us to take this journey together, so that you may understand what it meant then, and why in retrospect it means even more to me today.

To begin with, milk was one of the staples of our diet. Straight from the farm, unprocessed except for cooling, ours was always boiled before use – probably a necessary precaution in those days before tuberculin testing, when even the washing down of cows before milking might be sketchy. The country belief in "eating a peck of dirt before you die" was a handy trouble-saver! True, we felt that we suffered somewhat from parental caution when, on rare occasions of going out to tea, my mother would produce a medicine bottle of ready-boiled milk and explain apologetically that "the girls were used to it". There were traumas attached to the actual boiling process too. If we tried to hurry it by turning up the flame of the oilstove under the saucepan, a nasty burnt flavour would result at best, while at worst the whole house would be filled with the indescribable, penetrating smell of milk boiled over on the stove. Thundery weather could cause the whole day's supply to "turn" before one's eyes as a certain temperature was reached. But with all the hazards, milk we had to have, and having it came to mean fetching it.

I look back on two main phases in this fetching of the milk. Before "lessons" came to occupy the major part of weekdays, and before the deterioration of my father's health, there was a period when it was one of our "walks with Dad". And walks with Dad were usually fun, if a trifle breathless. He swung along with great strides, as befitted his height of six foot three, armed with a walking stick which struck the ground at every second stride, and which he raised in a rather gracious salute to anyone we met. I have often wondered about that walking stick; he must have enjoyed the feel of it in his hand, for in his walking days no-one ever needed a stick less. At one time we three had miniature ones too, and they lingered in the hallstand for many years. "Fetching Dad's stick" was a necessary prelude to a walk, and taking it up to the forge to have its iron ferrule renewed was an occasional exciting errand. The only real uses for it, however, were the hooking down of blackberry sprays and the shooting of imaginary rabbits (us, when very small) who would run hilariously on a few yards to drop dead in long grass. But I digress. Back to the fun element of fetching the milk with my father. He would stand while we scrambled up banks to climb on to the sawn off tops of tree stumps, and jumped daringly off them, heart in mouth, on to the grass verge below. He would wait, nay actively participate, while we searched through the piles of small stones deposited ready for road-mending – a fascinating source of the occasional tiny fossil, gleaming white quartz pebble or red-veined "dolls' meat stone". (I hope that the Highways Department did not miss the few legs of lamb or rounds of beef, that we purloined). During our scooter era he would stride ahead and stand on corners to beckon us on if the way was clear, and many were the competitions we enjoyed, starting from a given point to see who could travel the furthest without putting a foot to the ground. Start level, hold your handlebars, one, two, three, off! Push off as forcefully as you can, to get up the impetus and speed necessary for distance trials, then swoop along, steering in and out of the worst bumps and hollows in the road, with the wind in your face and the exhilaration of flying in your heart. On, on – but the pace slackens, the impetus wanes, all your skill is needed to shift your weight and keep the scooter moving as long as possible. No, it's no use – you come to a standstill, look round and laugh, and strike your foot on the ground again for another, this time non-competitive stretch. It was a joyous sport, if hard on the sole of one's left shoe, and even occasional collisions did not deter us in the least. My father carried the milk can, so no burdens hindered us. If scooterless, we had free hands for exploring the hedgerows and verges and carrying back the small treasures that took our fancy – dog-roses or sprays of hips, lichened twigs or autumn-tinted leaves. Why, oh why did the leaves so quickly become dry and brittle, losing their lovely colours and veinings almost before our eyes when we reached home, lingering dryly around for a day or two and then vanishing like a parable of mortality?

Just as the leaves vanished, so did this phase of milk-fetching come to an end. We were deemed responsible enough to go on our own, Phil in charge, with Susie or me alternately to accompany her on weekdays; at weekends I think all three of us went. And so began a routine which governed our days for some years. The ringing of the school bell at five minutes to nine is the signal for my mother, scattering last instructions for the preparation of vegetables for dinner, to disappear into school. Phil vanishes into the Front Room to do her daily piano practice, while Susie and I start to organize the clearing away of breakfast. Phil conscientiously puts in her allotted time at the piano, to be succeeded by her

appointed fellow-traveller of the day. There follows a painful
plodding through exercises, scales, and the current "piece" if
it is me, or a virtuoso performance if it is Susie. Phil
meanwhile locates the milk can, and calls up to my father (a
ritual, this) "Do we have to take our macks?" Almost
inevitably, unless we are in the middle of a heat wave or the
roof is sparkling with frost, his answer will be "Yes, I think
you'd better". I have only lately realized that this was due not

only to his natural caution and pessimism (for if you Got Wet you were sure to Catch Cold); he was judging the day, at that time of the morning, from the sunless side of the house, and our occasional mild protestations that "the sun's out at the back" did not convince him in the least.

So we were kitted appropriately, ready for departure. In winter there were our navy blue reefer coats, relieved by gilt buttons, anchor-embossed, and those navy-and-red tam-o'-shanters with the silk tassels, that I loved (as distinct from many of our clothes which I endured). As we outgrew these they were replaced by brown tweed mixture coats and home-knitted berets. Grey knitted gloves did their best to keep our hands warm – not very successfully in my case. Lengthening, warmer days meant permission to go without coats; and a delicious sense of freedom it was, after the constricting winter, to flex arms hampered by only two layers of home knitting – a pullover and what was then called a jersey-coat – even though the inevitable mack was probably dangling over one arm "just to be on the safe side". In the summer days to follow, cotton dresses would appear, or more likely reappear, with a bright tell-tale unfaded band at the bottom edge of the skirt where the hem had been let down. It was bliss to wear as little as this again, to walk in sandals instead of heavy winter shoes, with our bare legs freed from thick grey socks. I was never so keen on the linen hats we wore whenever there was any sun about, too much of it on one's head being considered Bad For One. I found mine hot and uncomfortable; and (a curious phenomenon we regularly observed), my hat, which was blue, seemed to attract insects, buzzing around it and even alighting to enjoy free rides, while Phil's yellow and Susie's green interested them not at all. Wet days entailed, of course, the actual wearing of those macks and their matching sou'westers, plus sturdy wellington boots. The macks were made of something like American cloth, with a shiny surface (when new) and a woven soft cotton underside. We seemed adept at collecting mud on them, so they had to be sponged down before each trip – it was permissible to come back with mud, lovely thick white chalky mud, on your mack, but not to set off, and the sponging would often be done, at top speed, by poor Phil during her companion's music practice.

If I linger on this physical preparation for the sortie, it is because it underlines for me one of the basic values inherent in going to fetch the milk. We experienced and learned to accept the inescapableness of the weather in its every mood and season, in a way that many of today's children do not. I have suggested earlier that one hardly deserves the ecstasy of awakening Spring unless one has felt the chill of Winter, really felt it in icy feet, numbed hands and tingling ears. A child who is whisked from a warm house by car into a warm school, who hardly sets foot outside till, as my mother used to say, "the streets have aired a bit", is deprived of both the agony and the ecstasy. I know, of course, that this is not true of many children today! And I am irrational enough, and sybarite enough, to rejoice now in my own warm house and car. All the same I am thankful that the rhythm of the seasons has worked itself deep into my bones and is a part of that by which I live. "While the earth remaineth, seed-time and harvest, and cold and heat, and summer and winter, and day and night shall not cease" – this is no empty promise to me, for I have seen it fulfilled day by day, season by faithful season, ever since I was aware of anything outside myself. We confronted the weather face to face; were nipped by the frost, transported by snow and rime, sock-sodden with driving rain streaming down our macks into our boots, caressed by the soft winds of Spring and buffeted by Autumn gales, bathed in grateful Summer heat. I have tasted it all and it is right and good, an eternal, unshakable verity, a living experience which nothing can take away.

So, equipped for our encounter, we set off. We will leave Susie behind today, to turn out the oilstove in the Front Room when her piano practice is over, reduce the lingering disarray of breakfast (one of our favourite breakfast dishes was, believe it or not, macaroni cheese, and it takes some washing-up), peel the potatoes, prepare the carrots, sprouts, leeks or whatever is in season. We will push to the back of our minds a nagging doubt as to whether she may, in the event, be found lost in a book among the still unwashed dishes when we come back, so that we shall all have to turn to in a mad rush to complete the routine jobs by the appointed time. Oblivion in a book is one of the family failings, but there is nothing we can do about it at this stage. "Just off" we call up the stairs to my father, and off we go, past the high windows of the Big Room of the school, where two little figures known to us as "angels learning to read" gravely support their burden of stone frames as they have already done for three quarters of a century and as they still do today, fifty years on. Through the window comes the thump and drone of chanted tables, the quiet buzz of children working at their books, or the joyful sound of the weekly singing lesson storing minds with melody to endure for years. Past the little bell tower from which the summons to school is called at five to nine and five to one, past the outdoor tap which was once, within our memories, the only water supply for both the school and the house; out of the white gate, turn right and we are really on our way. And – vital point number two – we are also on our own.

I do not know whether I have conveyed a picture of us as over-protected children, but certainly by today's standards, this is what we were. Prince Charles'* sheltered life had nothing on ours. There was an odd duality in the Grown-Ups' attitude towards us. Infinitely loved, valued, and cherished, we were expected to excel and to act responsibly, yet given very few opportunities for the latter. Things that the village children did as a matter of course – riding bicycles for instance – were closed to us as too dangerous, or too expensive, or both. We more or less accepted this, and if we desired more autonomy, it was as one desires the unattainable. But fetching the milk gave us a little slice of independence on a plate for forty minutes of each day, and it was a fearful joy. Fearful because we might have to make decisions, and they might afterwards prove to have been wrong; because even on this well-trodden mile there lurked perils known and unknown. But a joy, definitely a joy, to taste responsibility, to be ourselves, to show that we could safely perform this basic rite and come back in one piece, a mild but persistent assertion of ourselves as personalities that could exist away from the all-knowing, all-pervading Grown-Ups; and like the weather, it was good.

Out of the gate then, leaving on one side the village police station, and on the other, looking up to the glorious straggle of lilac and laurel which was our hedge on to the road. At other times we would clamber into its thick leafy depths, imagining ourselves unseen, bestriding the strong lower branches as mettlesome horses and emerging eventually with sleeves and shoulders streaked green from contact with the damp powdery lichen that covered every twig and bough. But now, pass Old Shep's ramshackle chicken-run, hearing maybe his soft Wiltshire burr mingle harmoniously with the clucking, crowing, cackling and croodling of the birds. Walk under the elm trees – green, yellow or bare – whose numbers we have, alas, seen reduced by storms; one even fell crashing into the playground, to flatten the iron railings and then lie with its treacherously shallow roots ignominiously exposed for several days, until sawn up and removed. Pass a magnificent "conker" tree, still enduring majestically today; under its spreading boughs stands, not the village blacksmith of poetic fame, but the old stable belonging to the pub and now housing the publican's hearse-like car which is also the village taxi. Look up and you will see on the wall a legend imprinted on my mind for ever, as a metal advertisement proclaims LACTIFER FOR CALVES. And now we are in the village proper, with its cluster of thatched cottages and little houses, its one pillar box set into the wall of the Vicarage kitchen garden, its glimpses of the Bridgemans' farm up on the right, and the church and manor standing tranquilly back from the road. We turn down the straight elm-lined stretch that we call the Avenue, leafy and pleasant but somewhat dull, with little but ivy and straggly grass competing with the elm roots for nourishment. After three hundred yards or so the lane turns abruptly right – hug the bank, or better still, climb a miniature ladder of exposed elm tree roots and negotiate the corner above traffic level, for there always might be a car coming, or a farm wagon leaving little room for anything else, or (on Monday and Friday) the Bus, leaving no room at all. And since this corner really was the scene of a fatal collision between a lorry and a motor cycle, and has therefore associations as dark and grim as the splotched surface of the road – probably only spilt tar, but I always felt it was blood – it behoves us to be really careful. We breathe more freely when the corner is turned and the road opens out a little; the trees crowd together less closely, the grass verges are wider, and the Three Gates appear – two of them on one side of the road and one on the other, forming a staging post on the route. At about this point, if I remember rightly, it is worth while to begin to look for the first flowers in their season. "The first celandine (or primrose, or violet, or beloved meadow cranesbill) should be here" we could say with the confidence born of annual experience – and it was.

Here is another of the essential values of going to fetch the milk. We came to know those verges and hedges yard by yard, with the kind of intimate, detailed, affectionate knowledge which can only be gained by making the same journey on foot, day in and day out, at all seasons, with one's eyes wide open. We were almost unwittingly making an ecological study that was more than superficial, though the word "ecology" had yet to arrive. Everything we saw we tried to identify; and the distribution of the flowers, their personalities from first leaf to seed-head, the changing aspect of the hedgerows with their bird, insect and small mammal population – all this became for us a precious and living pattern, a constantly shifting kaleidoscope in which each element had its rightful, interwoven and interdependent place. Almost we felt ourselves to be so much part of the fabric that without our daily scrutiny the cycle of growth would have been broken. There is a sweet security, a warm and poignant stab of recognition, in finding the earliest red campion bloom straggling up through the same hawthorn bush as ever, in seeing goldfinches on thistle heads exactly where you saw them last year and the year before, and where, please God, you will see them again next year. "While the earth remaineth…" Perhaps it is only given at one stage of a lifetime to have this experience in both its fullness and its minuteness; but I still need the reassurance of the seasonal cycle to keep me balanced and whole. I must plant bulbs in the Autumn with faith and hope, thrill to the first green leaves of even the humble nettle or cow-parsley, look for primroses (but in these days of progress I must not pick them); I must leap in spirit at the arrival of the earliest house-martin, smell new-mown hay in Summer and make blackberry-and-apple pudding every Autumn. I must keep in contact with my seasonal roots, as much and as far as I can, or I shall be no longer myself.

But we have only reached the Three Gates, not halfway as yet, and our time is limited. We must keep moving, along the gently winding stretch that lies before us, where ditches fill in the winter and sometimes overflow to lap halfway or more across the road. "The water was out today" is the accepted phrase for reporting this on arrival back home. Look well as you go, miss no tiny thing of interest with your well attuned eyes and mind, but press on to the next landmark, the Yellow Dogshed. It was pronounced, in fact thought, as I have written it, though reason would dictate Yellow Dog Shed, for it is a dilapidated shed or barn guarded by a yapping yellow dog. He is safely tied up (poor thing) but of course he always might get loose, so this is no place to linger. Another bend or two in the road, and a group of little houses appears – just three or four of them, sitting side by side at the top of a steep bank. Some of the dwellers here remember the days when their water had to be fetched from the main village, "and of course, my old Dad, he did always have a pint in the pub when he did go to fetch the water, so that were a dear bucket of water in those days". Now the road dips down a little hill and climbs up another – good scooter ground, this, in earlier days – and you may catch a sweet whiff of young calves, hear them gently lowing for their food, lean over a wall and look into their sad liquid brown eyes, perhaps even touch their soft ears and wet noses. For this is where our farmer rears his calves, the calves at whose expense (when you come to think of it) we are getting our milk. Here, often, is our farmer himself, in battered hat and khaki drill overall, his hefty boots encrusted with mud and dung, swinging himself over the wall, bucket in hand, after feeding or inspecting the calves. In the corner of his mouth is an incredibly short pipe ("to keep me nose warm in winter" as he once explained to us), which he whips out to give us his usual cheery greeting of "Good morning, young ladies, and 'ow are you this morning?" We know him well enough to have lost our shyness, and can greet him happily in reply. Up to the main farm now and into the cool damp dairy at the back, where we leave our empty milk can, pick up a full one, and set out on the return journey. Once a week there may be eggs to collect as well. I have never forgotten the one occasion when I dropped them halfway home, eggs being my portion while Phil carried the milk can. With what trepidation I told the Grown-Ups, and with what relief I accepted the mild injunction to be more careful in future! I felt that I had got off undeservedly lightly, knowing that eggs cost money, and money was scarce. The unpredictability of Grown-Ups was on my side for once. At other times I could be in deep trouble over something that seemed quite innocent to me, or obviously someone else's fault.

But what of the perils at which I have hinted? Some of them were foreseeable – we might, for instance, be waylaid by dear Old Shep at his chicken-run, and enmeshed in one of his endless, barely intelligible discourses. How to respond, how to escape without being rude? Further on the way there was a similar hazard in the person of Old William – another great talker who loved to hold us up. "Off for your little annual walk then?" he would begin (we never knew whether this was a joke or a misunderstanding of "annual"), and from this opening gambit he could carry on, it seemed, for ever. He once caused us acute embarrassment by producing two apples for us from the depths of his filthy coat pocket, polishing them on his well-used red handkerchief before handing them over. We knew that we would not have been allowed to eat them if a Grown-Up had been with us, but we didn't want to hurt his feelings. I think

Phil murmured something about "eating them later" and we hurried on, to "lose" them in a ditch when safely out of sight. Another peril for me was that harmless manure-cart which, you will remember, my wretched imagination insisted on transforming into a plague-cart. I would gulp inwardly, try not to look at its rich odoriferous load for fear of seeing a horrible, dangling, plague-stricken limb or head, and somehow force myself past it. I never told even Phil, of course – children are not much given to sharing their private horrors. Meeting people was another peril, though a diminishing one as we grew older and gained a little confidence, but at one time it was an agony of self-consciousness to greet even the most familiar figures in passing.

It would be unkind and untrue to include Phil's bird-watching propensities as a hazard – better perhaps to say that I found them trying at times. Her dedication was such that no flutter of a wing, no pipe, chirp or twitter escaped her, and anything unfamiliar must be followed up. I would be abruptly halted in my tracks and enjoined to silence and immobility by her authoritative whisper or pointing finger, while she crept off to stalk her bird. With my short sight I usually could not spot it anyway, and was certainly unable to note its finer points; impatient (as always) and bored, I would fidget as much as I dared, longing to hear her disappointed "It's gone now" and to be beckoned on again. Phil also had a habit, in damp-but-not-quite-yet-raining weather, of putting on her sou'wester without tying the strings of it under her chin. I chose to think this abominably untidy, and would dawdle along ten yards behind her, trying to look as if I didn't know her. To balance this, she objected strongly to my liking for the meadow sorrel which grew along the verges. Country children like to pick the young stems and chew them for their pleasantly sharp taste, spitting out the tough fibres when all the flavour is gone, and we were allowed to do this on walks in the fields with my father. No doubt Phil was right to think it too messy a procedure when we were on the road, but of course I wouldn't give in, and the air would be silently electric for a couple of hundred yards. But usually it was a harmonious expedition, one that further cemented relationships through more shared experiences. Unknown hazards had to be dealt with impromptu; and once survived, they fell into place in memory, tinged by satisfaction at the surmounting, but a little apprehension lest they should recur. An unusual fusillade of hoof-beats on the road once made us scramble hastily up the tree-root ladder, just in time to avoid a confrontation with a roguish-looking runaway cart-horse – what fright, or freak, had sent him trotting up the lane we never knew. Phil, fetching the milk by herself one day (most unusual) was accosted by a gipsy woman who asked whether that was cold tea she had in her can. "I said it wasn't and hurried on". Admirable handling of an emergency, we all agreed when we heard the tale. Horribly traumatic was the one time when we arrived at the Farm in the middle of a pig-killing – were we, for some reason, either early or late that day? I think we must have been, for it would have been most unlike our cheerful friend not to remember our daily arrival when planning the execution. Once, too, we were greeted by an empty can and told that there had been an accident and all the milk had been lost, so there was nothing for us. What we were deliberately and kindly not told was that one of the farmworkers had had a brainstorm and overturned all the milk churns; as we had to pass his cottage, our farmer, or his wife, thought we might be frightened to do so if we heard the full tale. I believe the man recovered and continued to work on the farm as before. In a happier category were Adventures. Occasionally we would be given a lift part of the way – permissible, of course, only if it was someone we knew. This meant (once) old Mr. Bridgeman's horse and trap, and from time to time, the Vicarage car. On very rare occasions, if the weather was really bad and it was a "Bus day" we might use the Bus in one direction – the time was convenient but this cost a whole penny each, a serious matter. The Bus would obligingly stop to pick us up at any point on the route – would even slow down invitingly without being hailed – but usually we had to wave it on. Adventures, however, were mostly sightings – a stoat or weasel streaking across the road, a stripe-faced badger rooting in a ditch, a jay or woodpecker (even I could see that), the huge odorous Goat Moth caterpillar we once found, the jewel-like orange fungi that sprouted from dead wood, or the huge plate-like ones on trees – any of these could make our day and give us a tale to tell when we returned.

And return we must, for we work to a programme. Watchless, we must gauge the time aright, and the mile back is usually taken at a brisker pace. Here is the roadman, with his hand-barrow of hoes, spades and such, at his endless task of trimming, tidying and sweeping, covering the whole parish on foot and making an amazingly good job of it – a couple of hundred yards further down the lane than when we met him twenty minutes ago. He is a man of few words, so a quick greeting will suffice. Are we late? Shall we have to pick our way through the cows returning to pasture after milking? – an encounter we often have to face but do not greatly relish. But today all is well. Phil shifts the heavy milk can (two quarts is quite a weight) from one arm to the other. The cottages are in sight again. By the wall of the Vicarage garden we pause, open a door, and pick up yesterday's copy of "The Times" which the Vicar kindly passes on to my father. In at the school gate and back into the house. Sigh with relief – Susie has resisted all temptation to read and greets us virtuously with

the table cleared and the potatoes peeled. We report our safe
return to my father and put the milk in its special saucepan
on the kitchen oilstove to boil. Watch it now, Susie – the
morning has gone too well to be marred by the reeking fumes
of a boil-over – while Phil and I prepare mugs of mid-morning
cocoa. The first child rushes triumphantly out into the school
playground for break, and my mother arrives to drink her
cocoa hastily, check that all is well, and give final instructions
for "putting on the dinner". Rushed as she is, she can still
listen to our account of the morning's journey, share our
excitement if there has been an Adventure, admire any
treasures we have brought back. Then she is gone again; the
playground hubbub dies abruptly at the sound of a whistle
and the children file back into school. It is time for our lessons
to begin too, and we brace ourselves for Latin, Geometry or
Algebra. We have made our foray into our mile-long kingdom
and are assured that all is well there. We have seen and felt

the almost imperceptible daily change and growth of the season, registered the tiny details of sight, sound and scent which make up our world. Once more we have taken it into our very selves, only later to realise what this most basic of experiences has done for us. We have had our forty minutes' worth of independence. And tomorrow, whatever the weather, we shall go to fetch the milk again.

---

* Prince Charles, while at University, is said to have come on stage during a student revue under an umbrella, saying "Hitherto I have led a very sheltered life".

I once had an older friend, a town-dweller but at heart a country-lover, who delighted to escape from her London suburb for long walks in Bucks or Surrey, and who would sit out in her garden wrapped in several rugs, late into the autumn, such was her passion for air and space. As a young teacher I shared her house for several years and helped to keep the garden under control. I discovered by chance, one damp day when fat suburban snails were a-creep among the London Pride, that she was incredibly ignorant – she did not know, had no idea, that a snail's eyes are those pinheads on the end of its horns. If this knowledge came as a revelation to her ("How clever of you to know things like that"), her ignorance was equally a revelation to me – how could anyone who had tended even a suburban garden, and walked in the country, all her life, not know things like that? I realized then that the lore of creatures great and small (and I include here flowers, which to me are as much alive as are living things that can move) is not something that comes naturally from just seeing. It is the result of the wise harnessing of children's natural curiosity from an early age by sensitive adults. This is as true of country children as of town ones; unless guided, they may take the wealth around them for granted, and carelessly use it for their own ends, unable to name the birds' nest they destroy or the rare flower they rip up and then toss away as heedlessly as their fathers

would plough it into the ground. In the Wiltshire of my childhood a bye-law made it an offence to uproot any wild flower, but to the best of my knowledge, that was as far as "conservation" (still an unknown term) extended.

How blessed we were, then, to have parents who helped us to perceive rather than just to see, who fed us with books and trained us to identify what we found, and who tolerated (in the main) our strange and messy "collections" and successive pets.

We learned to reverence life in its many forms. Pets must be fed and cared for properly. Flowers plentiful enough to be picked, as were most, had to be carried home carefully and put in water; in bluebell time we would sorrow over the wilting bunches we sometimes found, gathered greedily by others and then abandoned. We learned a life-long abhorrence of blood sports of all kinds. My mother waged war, with some success, on the country boys' unthinking habit of birds'-nesting, and many of her pupils learned from her to know and respect what they saw around them, so that a visiting school inspector with a passion for wild flowers could be safely dispatched up the Hill at lunch time, with a group of the older children to show her our local rarities. Susie's worm-deading activities would certainly have been firmly checked had Phil and I reported them to the Grown-Ups. The world of creatures great and small was our playground, but a playground to be enjoyed with respect.

I suppose, looking back, that in truth there was an element of exploitation mingled with our enjoyment when we were very small, though I know that I felt creative rather than destructive when making daisy-chains in country-child tradition, or collecting the pale pink bell-shaped flowers of the small bindweed which crept over the school garden plots. We pulled the blooms off the stems and then threaded them all on to a grass stalk to make a little flounced swag which we adored for a few minutes till something else claimed our attention. We made poppy-dolls in season – the scarlet Oriental poppies that grew by the steps up to the "little house" at the top of the garden were ideal for this. Choose a poppy in its prime and pick it, being careful not to smear the sticky juice from the stem on your would-be-clean dress, for it stains. Bend the petals carefully outwards and downwards, leaving the powdery black stamens exposed as the doll's hair; tie a grass-blade sash around the doll's waist, insert a grass stem for arms, and there is your poppy-doll. We improvised boats (laurel leaves from the front garden hedge, perhaps) and sailed the dolls on the old tin bath of water which was one of our happiest summer playthings, among those plantain-leaf-and-buttercup water-lilies which were another innocent bit of destructiveness. My mother taught us to cut off the heads of dandelions and slit the hollow stems lengthways for a couple of inches from each end – then put them in water and watch the slit ends curl up like springs. Our hands would be stained brown with the acrid milky juice and would need scrubbing with pumice stone at bedtime, but it was worth it. On dewy summer mornings we prowled along the row of Californian poppies which my mother usually grew, looking for the buds whose pointed covers, shaped like a dunce's hat, were parting from the base of the flower. We eased them gently off to see the newborn petals unfold – yellow, orange, creamy white or bronze-red. And as the tall aquilegias (columbines to us) dropped their purple, pink or yellow horns we were there to collect them, sort them and compare them for size and beauty. You might shake the plant very gently to see if any more were ready to fall, but honour (and the Grown-Ups) demanded that nothing was "collected" before its time. Supreme happiness of childhood! this joy in tiny, delicate, natural things, as we looked minutely on our world and saw that it was good.

There was a wealth of such treasures to be gleaned from both the garden and the school playground. We grew Jerusalem artichokes, whose tall stems when dried to silver-grey crackliness contained an interesting core of white pith. We called this sugar-cane, and enjoyed stripping off the dead outer casing to see who could produce the longest unbroken stick of "pure sugar-cane". And we spent happy hours collecting "seed-pearls" in the playground. These were really the seeds of the ivy which grew up our three hawthorn trees; its berries, not to be eaten by us, gave a feast in season to flocks of chattering, chirring starlings who spat out the seeds for us to gather. Exquisite, tiny, and precious they were – pearly white or stained pink – bounty for eager small hands to collect and sort, and hoard for a day or two until they shrivelled away. We tried to make elderberry wine by soaking and stirring ripe elderberries – purple fingers this time – in "seaside pails" of water – a lovely game, though the dingy liquid that resulted was unappetizing even to the dolls. More successful were our attempts at making scent from rose-petals, or from the fragrant feathery leaves of the "old man" (better know as "lad's love") which grew at the top of the little rockery. Both yielded some kind of fragrance, at least for a day or two, though Phil's attar of roses ended up smelling more like our old friend Owbridges' Lung Tonic than anything else, and my father once incurred my wrath by accidentally throwing away my precious bottle of scent. As it was well past its prime, I had later to concede that perhaps he couldn't have been expected to know that it was important…… Further afield, there was all the berried wealth of the hedgerows. Ruby red haws could safely be nibbled by our small teeth; the thin edible layer round the hard little stone had a not unpleasant mealy flavour, though the real attraction was the feeling of partaking in wild-growing bounty. Flaming hips, cut through, revealed seeds neatly packed in a silky fibre; country children call this "itchy powder" and try to drop pinches of it stealthily down each others' backs, just as they like to creep up with burrs that cling tight to jackets and jerseys, or lengths of goose grass to wind round the socks of unsuspecting friends – and how it clings! Slate blue sloes we admired, but one bite of the bitter-tasting things was enough for us. Beech and hazel nuts were ours to gather and eat, even sweet chestnuts if we took the walk to the "swinging trees". Here also we could find acorns with exciting shaggy cups to add to our "collections" of ordinary acorns turning from green to brown in some tolerated corner at home, together with conkers gradually, alas, losing their first glossy bloom and drying away to dull hardness. What miracles of creation were the outer cases of both the sweet and the horse-chestnuts – prickly or spiky outside and silk-smooth within, satisfying equally the eye and the hand of childhood and carrying with them the astringent tang of the fallen leaves among which we scrabbled to find them. As nostalgic and evocative as the sounds of the country are its scents and smells. A whiff of fallen leaves, or new mown hay; the smoke of a bonfire, even the distinctive down to earth smells of healthy animal dung – horse, sheep, cow and chicken, to say nothing of pig, each has its own aroma – and I home back unerringly into the right season and setting, fifty years gone in a flash.

I fear that the urge to capture was in us as in all young children – try to convince any three-year-old that ladybirds are happier free than confined in his matchbox, and you are up against something really primitive. Perhaps the Grown-Ups were unaware of some of our activities at the far end of the garden, at the stage when we were still learning the lesson of complete respect. The snails – plump, horny garden ones or exquisite smaller field-dwellers with delicate cream, pinky-brown or black-and-white spirally striped shells – which were among our early captives, did not really have a very good time. Too many of them came to a nasty squashy end with the collapse of the "lovely houses" we built for them from pieces of old roof tiles precariously balanced on sticks, and they must have grown very bored with their monotonous diet of dandelion leaves. Luckily for them, they were adept at escaping by night, so that one often found "my BEST snail" gone in the morning. I remember also catching bees in jam jars, where they buzzed furiously round and round making the jars echo to their frustration; some of them, alas, did not manage to escape. When in the course of my training as a teacher I encountered William James' famous description of the impact of the world on the senses of a newborn baby as "a booming, buzzing confusion", I knew exactly what he meant – a noise like a bee in a jam jar.

Collections of caterpillars led, I think, to some firmer instruction in providing the correct food for one's pet. We were not encouraged to keep the caterpillars which infested our cabbage plants (and oddly, the same ones would eat the sharp-tasting leaves of nasturtiums just as greedily) – there were far too many of them already, and the appearance of the first "Cabbage White" butterflies, though a landmark in Spring, was technically not supposed to be welcomed. (Once, and only once, I killed a butterfly in defence of the cabbage towards which it was fluttering with egg-laying intent; the act filled me with such revulsion that I hated myself for days, and never repeated it). But interesting caterpillars could be found on hawthorn or ragwort, and some of these we kept for days on end, well supplied with their own chosen food. And Woolly Bears! They were everywhere in the summer, hurrying from one plant to the next, deliciously furry to handle (no-one thought about allergic rashes in our childhood, so we didn't have them), willing to crawl ticklingly up bare arms and to perform hazardously on tightropes of wool stretched between two sticks. I can't recall keeping any of them long, though – they seemed to have a hasty nature and were soon on their way. Best of all was the Puss Moth caterpillar which we once acquired, a fascinating creature with a face rather like that of a cat, and an apple-green body ending in a short forked tail from which, if "Kitty" was annoyed, two red whip-like threads would appear, to lash furiously about. We reared "Kitty" successfully on fresh leaves from the willow trees whence she had come, provided her with dead wood on which to pupate, and saw her emerge in Spring to fly away as a furry, grey-white, adult Puss Moth.

On summer evening walks we could find the pale yellow, almost transparent chrysalises of the Burnet Moth bending the tips of long grass stems, and often we watched a moth emerge, damp and trembling, then dry and unfold its red and black wings and take to the still warm air. It is a sad fact, not a nostalgic fancy, that butterflies and moths were far, far more plentiful in those days before chemical pollution of fields, hedges and verges. The vivid yellow Brimstone Butterfly was usually the first to announce the coming of Spring. Red Admirals and Painted Ladies were ten a penny, Orange Tips a somewhat rarer sight. The entrancing Small Blue was everywhere, its food plants thriving in our chalky soil. Magpie Moths fluttered among the gooseberry bushes. Marbled White and Tortoiseshell, Speckled and Wood Butterflies were ours in plenty; we are all diminished by their scarcity or even, alas, extinction, little dreamed of then.

Small creatures of many kinds could be sighted fleetingly on our walks, scuttling across the lanes or along the ditches. Tiny dead things we learned to accept – pathetic naked baby birds, or the shrews and mice which our cats would capture, play with, kill and abandon. Country cats will go for almost anything that flutters or runs, whether eatable or not. Ours would hunt frogs, rabbits and birds as well as the mouse population, and every Spring we had to go through the process of first loathing and then forgiving them for it. A succession of injured or abandoned fledglings taught us the sad lesson that one can seldom, without really expert knowledge, save these wild waifs, though we tried very hard.

Once a sparrowhawk, wounded in the breast but still just alive, dropped into the garden; obviously past help, it snapped a feeble defiance at us from its fierce beak as its yellow eyes glazed over and it gasped its way into death. I suppose we buried it with due honours. The cats occasionally brought home a mole – an exquisitely formed little creature, grey velvet coated, with tiny shovel-like hands and feet – to be mourned over briefly, examined closely ("don't touch it, it might have INSECTS") and then disposed of. But hedgehogs defeated the cats, so they trundled around freely at night and sometimes even allowed us a glimpse of their weird prickly forms by day. And luckily the cats never touched the Old Shed Toad – that leathery, warty friend who was with us for many years, emerging from the depths of the shed to clamber laboriously up and around the rockery stones, where no doubt he found juicy slugs to his heart's content. He was part of the family scene. I return in memory to summer evenings, warm and dusky, the white jessamine under the window filling the air with sweetness and the dew beginning to fall…… creep out quietly with a candle lantern (for "electric torches" have not yet reached us) and you may catch a glimpse of him, scrambling about his business. The Old Shed Toad is here on cue, just as he should be on this kind of evening, at this point in the rolling yearly cycle. All is well; blow out the lantern, and we can go satisfied to bed.

In spite of their lower nature, we could not have imagined our home without cats. The first I can remember was Mike, or Big Puss, a large ginger and white tom – a great rabbit-catcher who would come home literally bulging like a barrel after a successful hunt, perhaps dragging a horrid gory half-carcase which he had been unable to finish. It seems to be instinctive with cats to bring their trophies indoors if possible, so he would be greeted with discouraging cries of "Shut that door" and "Keep that cat out." No doubt he thought us very unappreciative of his prowess. In country fashion we put our cats out for the night (my mother assured us that they knew plenty of nice warm places in which to sleep), and fed them little, expecting them to forage for themselves. But we loved them dearly none the less, though Mike was a bit unapproachable – perhaps he had endured too much from us when we were very small. He was joined by Little Puss, otherwise Kotick (after Kipling's white seal) – albino and supposedly deaf, a more amenable character who could sometimes be stroked into submission enough to be dressed in dolls' clothes and wheeled in our old wooden dolls' pram, though even he would quickly fight his way out, leaving us to suck scratched fingers. But he was not with us long – did two cats prove too many? (though later on we had three). Given away, he found his way back at least once – a long and triumphant meow, a meow such as we had never heard before, announced his return late one night when we were in bed. We petted and fêted him the next morning and hoped that he would be allowed to stay, but he was firmly dispatched away again, to our secret sorrow. I can't remember the end of Mike Big Puss. Perhaps he met the all too common fate of a country cat – a trap or the gun of a gamekeeper – but we did have him till quite a ripe old age. Then came the three-cat era – how nice for the girls to have a kitten each! It was bliss. The kittens were fed on bread and milk till they were able to fend more or less for themselves. They slept in a basket in the kitchen while small, and were watched, tended, loved and played with endlessly – chasing woolly balls, pouncing deliciously after cotton reels pulled on a string, or one's moving finger tips on the ground. See them crouch and sight their blazing eyes on the target, start to twitch their tails and waggle their hindquarters – faster, faster, faster, and then the rush and pounce, the capture of your fingers by the still harmless little teeth and pin-pricking claws. Clever kitten! Catch it up in an ecstasy of love and possession, let it push its damp nose under your chin, purring its very soul out ("Don't let that kitten near your face" if a Grown-Up is about) – oh yes, the kittens were real joy, at least to Phil and me. But poor Susie's Blackie just disappeared early in his career; his little tabby successor succumbed to pneumonia in spite of my mother's care (she made him a pneumonia jacket and sat up all night with him), and a saddened Susie gave up hope of ever raising a kitten. Meanwhile Phil's rather wispy, pale-ginger-all-over, reticent Mike-the-second, and my frankly vulgar, cheerful, adored and adoring ginger-and-white Bill, flourished and lived to (I think) eleven and fifteen years old respectively. The last in the procession of cats was Whiskey, a wild-living black-and-white animal who was gradually persuaded to attach himself to us, and slowly, very slowly, became trusting enough to allow us near him. He is the only cat I have ever seen bathed – he once arrived home after an absence of several days, filthy, slimy and reeking of sewerage; what he had fallen or been thrown into was all too obvious. My indomitable mother filled the old tin baby bath with warm soapsuds, carried it outside, gritted her teeth and bathed him – after which he was dried on an old towel and restored to the family circle. He lived some years after that, gradually mellowing; it was a great day when we first coaxed a reluctant, throaty purr from him; and he was duly mourned when, mangled by a trap, he had to be sent to his last home.

Dogs we longed for, but never had. I remember a doggy phase when we pored over pictures of different breeds and selected which we would like to have, some mythical day in the future. Phil was long faithful to the idea of a Samoyed, and I hankered after an Afghan Hound, whose almost human face framed by long hair had a curious appeal for me. There was a brief rabbit (real rabbit) era, when a handsome sandy-coloured fellow called Bertram lived in an outside hutch. I think he soon came to be considered too smelly and was given away. At another time there were pigeons – pretty things who would stand still while we stroked their smooth-feathered heads, and who stayed with us long enough to breed. We watched their courtship; the male bird, with tail fanned out and one wing extended to brush the ground, circles the female uttering rapturous, excited coos in a crescendo of desire. Flattered but smug, she pretends at first to ignore his passionate invitation, but the performance soon degenerates into an undignified scramble to mate. In due course a clutch of eggs is brooded and the "squabs" hatch out. They deserve their awkward-sounding name, for they are ugly little things, like most young birds, till their scanty down, indecently naked skin and spiky growing feathers turn into a proper covering. But the feeding process is fascinating to watch – a baby bill opens wide, a parent one is thrust well inside, and by means of a visible pumping action the half-digested contents of the parent's crop is transferred to that of the little one. I think it was their persistent cooing, musical though we three considered it, which came to be felt an irritation and led to their departure.

And then, chickens! I have already tried to convey something of the joy of chicken-watching. To stand on a warm Spring or Summer day with face pressed as close as possible to the wire-netting round Miss Bridgeman's chicken-run (and what a satisfying visual pattern chicken wire makes, when you have all day to look at it) – to listen to the contented or excited sounds of the birds, to watch them scratch and scrabble among glinting golden straw on half bare earth – to feel the benison of the sun on your back as they do on their black, white, brown, gold, chequered or barred feathers (for

they are a gloriously variegated, motley collection); to see them go about their daily business of living and laying, each in its own observable, characteristic way – all this gave me some of the most magical, half drowsy, supremely contented moments of my early childhood. When later on the school poultry-keeping began and we also acquired our very own hens, it was fun, it was splendid, exciting and absorbing; but the sheer bliss of chicken-watching was something quite different, left behind in those light hearted dream days long ago, but still gratefully to be recaptured even now at the toss of a red comb, the glint of bronze and bottle green feathers or the gentle croodling of contentment from some lucky free-ranging denizen of a good old fashioned farmyard. Truly, as Evelyn Underhill has it –

"I come in the little things
Saith the Lord".

Little things! Tiny day-old chicks, darting out on heroic yard-long forays away from their clucking guardian hen whose distraught head pokes jerkily between the confining bars of the brooding coop. (Mother hens are reminiscent of inexperienced Sunday School teachers on an outing, obsessively counting their charges all day long). Or we might be privileged to see a batch of incubator hatched chicks, a hundred or more nestling together in the warmth of a central lamp and each others' bodies. We would scent their sweet clean fragrance, perhaps hold one briefly cupped in gentle hands, feel the strength of perfect, minute clawed feet and the tremor of a fast-beating little heart, brush our cheeks against soft primrose coloured down, and return the cheeping baby with a sigh to its place in the cosy throng. A pity, we felt, that chicks had to grow up, sprouting quills messily first on the wing-tips and then here, there and everywhere – becoming long-necked and rangy. Like lambs and kittens, calves, foals, piglets and children, they were at their most attractive when innocently small.

But I must celebrate the different pleasure of having our own hens, for an enormous pleasure it was. It came as an adjunct to my mother's school poultry-keeping – a piece of the neighbouring field having been acquired and a couple of the school garden plots sacrificed, there was room for a little private enterprise as well. With what eagerness we pored over books from the County Library – "Profitable Poultry-Keeping", "Backyard Poultry for Beginners" and such like; studied articles and advertisements as to different breeds, updated the scraps of poultry lore we had gleaned from Miss Bridgeman, discussed the merits of dry mash as against wet mash feeding! There must have been an unwonted release of funds to start us off. My father was an amused spectator, but along with my mother, whose enthusiasm could always be relied on, we were deeply and most enjoyably involved. Our conversation was soon full of breed names; solemnly we debated the virtues of Light and Heavy, the pros and cons of crossing them. The names are a delight to me still – Leghorns and Rhode Island Reds, White Sussex, Wyandottes of every shade, Anconas, Buff Orpingtons and Plymouth Rocks – we could rattle off the finer points of these well-known breeds, and were even knowledgeable about rarities like Frizzles, Silkies and Game Fowl. Little chicken houses of our own were bought or constructed. "Sittings" of eggs of our finally chosen breeds were acquired, broody hens hired, chickens hatched and reared. I remember my mother's choice of Exchequer Leghorns, supposed to embody all possible poultry virtues; Phil's attractive Silver Campines, and a temperamental Black Leghorn of mine called Petronella (for all our birds had names). But best of all were the bantams which became Susie's and my speciality – Ferdinand, a little cockerel whose fiery character more than made up for his diminutive size, and his two charming wives, speckled Isabella and brown Belinda. Their appetites were modest, their eggs (they laid profusely) large in comparison with their body size; and we were privileged to sell them to "the housekeeping" by weight, two ounces of bantam egg giving us the price of one ordinary egg. The bantams maintained a somewhat precarious financial balance, unlike the white Aylesbury duck which we fancied, but kept for a short time only; his appetite was such that he shovelled his way through our resources like lightning, with no foreseeable prospect of a return. For years I cherished a secret dream of finding a way to "bantamize" ducks, but it was obviously a project that could last a lifetime, and a dream it has remained. Bantams were best. I shall never forget the first hatching of eggs from our very own trio. Did you know that baby chicks destined to grow into speckled or otherwise multicoloured birds have striped backs and heads? Those eggs of ours produced the most enchanting collection of miniature chicks imaginable – one or two plain yellow, but the rest striped in shades of gold, brown, cream and rusty black. Alas, again, that they left the downy ball stage behind so fast! But our pride in rearing them was great, our joy at their first eggs immense. I don't know how long our poultry-keeping phase lasted; but I rank it as an important one in our lives, and I do know that we extracted every possible shred of experience, responsibility and enjoyment from it. Of course we were sentimental about our birds – they were pets first and foremost. We mourned over the inevitable losses and deaths, over the need to dispose of surplus young cockerels (to other peoples' tables, never our own); and if we occasionally cleared our expenses for a week or two, that was a bonus; any dreams we might have entertained of trebling our pocket money by "Profitable Poultry-Keeping" were quickly dispelled. Our birds lived happy lives, as far as one can judge, with clean quarters, regular feeding, and space to roam and scratch, and they will always have an honoured place in my remembered panorama of creatures great and small.

I have dwelt on the small rather than the great, for naturally it was with the smaller that we had the most sustained contacts. But the greater, as represented by the farm animals all around us, are an integral part of my childhood country landscape. The mechanization of farming had so far only produced the threshing machine which lumbered from farm to farm, steam-powered, when the corn harvest was in; for the rest, it was good old-fashioned horse-power. So the sunlit fields owed their even furrows to that ancient harmony between man and beast, the horse-drawn plough. Horses pulled the harrow, the haycutter, the reaping and binding machine which in a day transformed a whispering golden field into a stubbly expanse dotted precisely with stooks of drying sheaves. They carted everything from the newly dried hay, fragrant on its way to the stack, to the rigid black and white corpse of a cow which we once met on its way to its last resting place – not a fragrant memory, this. Patiently they stood on frosty early mornings when their every breath was a visible puff into the biting air, while the men cut frozen kale to be lugged down to waiting sheep or cattle. Their iron-shod, shaggy-fringed hooves endlessly plodded the miles of field, track and lane; massive shoulders and haunches rippled with heaving muscles as they strained up hills or over rough ground; heavy heads bowed low in effort, then were proudly raised as level ground was reached and the cart, wagon or machine ran more easily. A backward look at the wheels of the period, iron-girt or solid cast-iron, heavy and unyielding, makes me marvel again at such strength and endurance, just as I marvelled when small

– from a safe distance, for I always felt that, docile though the horses looked, they simply might not notice anything as insignificant as a four-year-old. I mourn their disappearance from the farm landscape (though I do accept the distant hum of a tractor as a genuine country sound these days); praise be that today's children can at least see in a "country park" or farm museum what I took for granted as a child – a working farm horse.

There were slenderer horses on some of the farms too, for riding or for the hunting which we came to loathe. But one could not but admire the horses. I recall one "Patsy" who belonged to our farmer; she would take fresh green grass (always better from outside her own field) from our slightly nervous hands, blowing softly in thanks and arching her gleaming neck to reach down to us. When she broke a leg hunting and had to be shot, we grieved for both a friend and a landmark. The foxhounds were attractive in their own way, if one could forget their purpose in life. One of my old writing books records laboriously that "A lost foxhound came to our back door" – a piece of excitement which I can recall. No doubt some obliging pupil at the school was pleased to take the disorientated, floppy-eared, black-tan-and-white-coated creature back to kennels, while I struggled with all those o's in my writing copy, whose tops obstinately refused to join up smoothly and neatly as they should.

Cows I remember as an interesting collection – white, rich brown, cocoa-coloured splashed with white, black or black and white, and the occasional red-gold of a Jersey or gold-brown of a Guernsey. We liked to watch them go by on their way to or from milking, but were less happy if we had to encounter them more directly on our journey for the milk. Bulls in those days were closely confined, in shed or high-walled pen, so we only rarely glimpsed one, led by an experienced cowman by a pole hooked through the ring in the bull's nose – a method of control taken as a matter of course. Calves, born out in the fields as calves should be, were appealing, and in the farm pens where they were later reared, friendly and approachable – over a wall, of course. Crossing open fields with cows in them always made me glance round nervously – cows are inquisitive, and if one takes it into her head to wander across and inspect the visitors to the pasture, the whole herd will follow; we knew of children who had actually been chased by cows, but fortunately we never suffered this ourselves. Phil, at least, overcame her fears enough to become really interested in cows and loved especially the soft-eyed, almost deer-like Jerseys and the white-muzzled Guernseys. Our childhood was full of the sounds of cows and milking – the lowing of herds on the move, the clamorous noise of young calves eager for their food, the sad distraught bellowing of the mothers when the calves were first taken away from them, the clang of pail and churn from the Bridgemans' neighbouring farm. Best of all was the occasional sleepy "moo" from a cow at night, momentarily disturbed perhaps by rabbit, fox or badger and then settling down again – a lovely sound that to me signified "All's well". There was bleating, grunting and squealing too, for most farms were mixed and had their sheep and pigs as well as dairy herds. Sheep tended to be kept on the higher ground up the Hill; we met them often on our walks across the fields, and I used to think that "silly sheep" described them perfectly, with their foolish, perpetually nibbling faces, their nervous starts away from us and their mindless crowd panics. But they were part of the scene, and one valued them just for that. Obligingly they left tufts of greasy wool on barbed wire for us to gather; they were mysteriously said to be "good for the mushrooms" (it took me a long time to realize how), and of course they produced the lambs which are of the essence of Spring. Sooty-faced and black-legged, their woolly coats suggesting a rather badly-knitted vest, they belong with the first celandine, the clean cold winds of early March, dangling hazel catkins and the first butterfly. No creature feels Spring madness more than do lambs, and they know how to express it, in sudden leaps and bounds, in zany charges and dashings, in posturings on top of hillocks and in frantic rushes back to the tolerant ewes to suckle in a butting, wriggling, orgiastic frenzy. Yet for all the lambs' *joie de vivre* there is a note of pathos in their high tremulous bleating, echoed by the deeper melancholy resignation of their mothers' voices – a subtle hint of loneliness and mortality.

There is nothing subtle about pigs, though. Every sound they make is frank and down to earth – greedy squealing and loud clamorous grunting for their food, sensuously contented noises as they dig into it, or, full and momentarily satisfied, waddle around the sty; high-pitched squeals of frustration or fright – you can never mistake a pig's meaning. From a distance they look jolly beasts, with humour in their turned-up snouts, cheeky ears and irresistible curling tails; it is only when seen closer that their rather mean little eyes belie the general impression of bonhomie. But mean or not, they were part of the scene, though I fear that theirs was a scene dirty to the point of squalor. It was assumed that pigs liked dirty conditions, and their sties were usually at least knee deep (pig's knee, I mean) in muck. The newly born silky piglets, till they were let out of the farrowing pen to join the general mêlée in the sty, looked all the sweeter and pinker by contrast, but this innocent freshness was short-lived, and their basic piggy natures were evident from the start as they lay greedily milking their mother, ten or twelve little bodies in a row, or learned to push and slurp at the feeding trough alongside their bad-mannered elders.

Lastly, from pigs back to wild flowers, which may perhaps seem an incongruous transition. But when I look back with love on our country kingdom I see that it was good simply because the creatures were what they were. The jolly vulgarity of the pigs was their quintessence, and as basically right as the qualities I came to value in the wild flowers which were part of our wealth. And what wealth of them there was, all around us in those days! The hay fields were mostly "old meadows", long undisturbed save by their annual mowing, and rich with the accumulated seed and root store of centuries. The hedgerows had stood since the days of enclosure or before, trimmed or re-laid by hand (what a work of art is a well-laid hedge, and what a horrible contrast is the massacre so often inflicted by mechanical hedge-trimmers today); and the verges beside them bloomed almost as freely as the meadows. The woods and copses, with minimum but sufficient management, gave shelter to their own shade-loving species; and the wide open downs, gently grazed by generations of sheep, had their own range of treasures. To walk over downland turf, so close and springy that your tread is tireless even after the three miles of hard road that you must cover first to reach it – to see the myriads of tiny plants crowding through the fine grass, offering their blooms defiantly, it seems, as soon as the sheep have passed by – to revel in the unique colour of miniature blue milkwort or yellow hawkbit, never so brilliant as on chalk soil – to scent the aromatic fragrance of the downs, feel the sun and hear the larks overhead – all this, to me, was very heaven.

And, praise be, it still is. I look back with thankfulness on the sheer profusion of the wild flowers of my childhood – bounty which few of today's children will know. Not for them the full richness of the seasonal succession in field and hedgerow, the intoxication of primroses by the fistful or a tossy-ball of cowslips. A child now, unless fortunate enough to live in one of the few "unspoilt" remote areas left to us must have his flowers meted out by visits to nature reserves (thank Heaven for conservation!) and must learn not to pick what were once the commonest of flowers. But although the profusion is largely now a memory for me, it is like the memory of a piece of music so well loved as to be part of my deepest self even if I should never hear it again, something that cannot be taken from me. I can still mark the seasons by their flowers, albeit fewer and more scattered than fifty years ago. The timeless perfection of plant form will never cease to move me to grateful wonder; the finding of a new flower, the greeting of a familiar one in an unexpected setting, still stirs me to the depths. The crowning legacy of my country childhood is the eternal message of the wild flowers, holding me in harmony with creation and saying "The Creator is good".

The Cat's got the Measles

A very odd sight this would be, I used to think, after my mother had introduced us to what we thought a hilariously daring verse, sung to the tune of "Weel may the keel row" –

The cat's got the measles, the measles, the measles,
The cat's got the measles
And I don't know what to do.

Incidentally I visualised the original as "We'll may the keelrow", thinking that a keelrow was some kind of wheeled contraption and that "may" in this context must mean "push"; "my laddie" was a flaxen-haired little boy of three or four. But the cat, the smitten cat, could only be our white Kotick all covered with bright red spots, which was a truly bizarre image.

Perhaps it was only a little less odd than the episode of our real measles, with which I might as well begin a round-up of events which have refused to be pigeon-holed elsewhere. One of my mother's stories of her own childhood was of measles, caught by two sizable families of cousins when staying together. It was a riotous tale of games and pranks during the enforced incarceration, of spotted boys climbing out of windows and wriggling along sills to visit spotted girls (in all innocence, I hasten to add) and – a detail which greatly fired my imagination – of endless drinks of liquorice water, made by shaking a bottle containing water and pieces of liquorice bootlace. One of the great disappointments of my young life was the discovery that liquorice is a flavour which I simply cannot endure............

And our measles were also a disappointment. We had had chicken-pox and whooping-cough, of which I have only hazily unpleasant memories; and in general, we were reared on the robust principle that being ill and staying in bed were things that just didn't happen to us. After a nocturnal "bilious attack" one might spend the next morning in a "chair bed" made by putting the two knobbly armchairs from the Front Room seat to seat, but that was about all. So I was shattered to be told one morning that we had all got measles and would have to stay in bed, especially as at that point I was not feeling in the least ill. I remember that I wept (another thing that was "not done" in our family) and had to be comforted and told that it really would be quite fun – we would have each others' company, and all our toys, perhaps even the cats, in bed, and how jolly it would be to compare our spots.

But it wasn't at all jolly. To this day I do not know how "Trowbridge" got wind of the fact that the Headmistress's children were down with measles, or why this was considered to be a danger to the school. But it was decreed that my mother must either take leave of absence without pay, or move out of the house and not see us for a specified period. An ignorant complaint from someone perhaps, met by bureaucratic stupidity? Of course forfeiting pay was unthinkable, so my poor mother had to sleep at a friendly farmhouse, and we were parted from her for the first time in our lives. The kitchen oilstove was moved out into the shed, and my mother cooked there in the evenings, holding that this did not constitute entering the house; doubtless she did the washing too, before pedalling off down the road to her enforced quarantine. My father was left with the role of nurse, which he discharged most faithfully – remember that he had been accustomed to the care of us while my mother was in school, from the time we were a few months old. I suppose we all made the best of it – a family tradition again – but it was very little fun for anyone, though there were a few lighter moments. I recall that one of us, having "just popped out of bed for a minute" in the middle of a meal, accidentally sat in someone's plate of mince on her return, which caused mingled apprehension and mirth. There was a most imaginative present from the farm where my mother stayed – a clump of snowdrops, lifted when just showing their white tips and planted in a bowl for us to enjoy. I remember this as an experience of real beauty. And there was our first taste of grapefruit – another present – which we tried

to eat like oranges and voted "horrible". There are long-lasting memories of ablutions at my father's hands, much too vigorous for our liking. How did we pass the time? I see a piece of board on which I pasted small pieces of wallpaper friezes that took my fancy – wallpaper books were quite a resource; and I have dim memories of preparing some kind of "Welcome Home" notice for the evening of my mother's return. In the event, however, I celebrated it by producing a whole new crop of spots and being really ill; but having served her statutory period of absence my mother firmly stayed put. Educational bureaucracy was surely at its pettiest and most stupid over this episode; "Trowbridge" retained an unpleasant aura in our minds for many years to come.

Tea at the Vicarage was an occasional event which gave us much enjoyment, as well as some anxiety, in anticipation perhaps even more than on the actual occasion. My father tended to shun "going out" more and more as the years went by, but he got on well with the old Vicar – that kind lender of "The Times" with a passion for his garden and for the antiquities of Wiltshire. This, and a shared love of wild flowers, furnished some common ground, so that when a state invitation, well-nigh a royal command, for the whole family was received, he would comply. For us three, going out to tea was a treat indeed. We hardly needed enjoining to be on our best behaviour; from the day of the invitation onwards we would be reminding each other of the smallest possible points of etiquette, as well as speculating on what we might eat, what we might do or have shown to us. Needless to say, the life-style at the Vicarage was very different from ours. My mother claimed that the chance to use a flush toilet was the major treat for us. But I remember the visits in terms of splendour – a loaded tea-table (I once covered myself with confusion by asking for "one of those little biscuits" and being told that they were pats of butter), Persian and Turkey carpets, massive and gleaming furniture, a shaggy hearth rug in front of a great open fire, and two droopy-eared spaniels to complete the picture. The Vicarage daughters entertained us girls after tea, with kindness and imagination. They seemed to us old and a little awe-inspiring, although they were in fact younger than our parents. But they would play "Old Maid" and "Snap" with us, or show us quaint and pretty things out of tall curio cabinets; once we were conducted round the conservatory, warm, fragrant, and jewelled with strange and lovely flowers. Many years later and shortly before her death I visited one of the daughters, really a very old lady by then, and we reminisced happily about the old village days. She remembered our visits and said that I had cut the conservatory down to size by calling it "a cosy little place" – showing off again, I fear. And was it after one of these occasions, or after an even rarer visit to the farmhouse, that I remarked that "they must be very rich because they seemed to have cake for tea every day"?

Another event, which shaped my looks if not my personality, was the discovery of my genuine myopia, somewhere between four and five years of age. Complaints that I couldn't see the blackboard in school had tended to be disregarded, but when one day my father decided to teach me to tell the time, my insistence that I really could not see began to convince him. I remember that he moved me nearer and nearer to the clock till I was almost on top of it and that when my mother came in from school he told her "I believe Alison really can't see properly". There followed cogitations, and eventually a visit to an optician in Swindon. I enjoyed every minute of this – any outing was a treat, and it put me one up on Phil and Susie. In the optician's waiting room I was much impressed by the first gas fire I had ever seen; and he was impressed, or pretended to be, because I could already write my name. On the way home in the dark, (someone had kindly taken us by car, for this was before the era of the Bus) we saw a blazing haystack with a fire engine in attendance, which seemed a bonus laid on for my special benefit. Back in our dim candle-lit kitchen I greeted Phil and a small sleepy

Susie with dramatic cries of "Haystack! Fire! Fire-engine!" but my entrance fell somehow a little flat – maybe they felt that I had had enough of the limelight for one evening.

In due course, round and nickel-rimmed arrived the first of various successive pairs of glasses, or "specs" as they were known in our family, and after a short spell of bewilderment I began to enjoy and take for granted a clarity of vision I had never had before. There were a few restrictions involved. I must stop trying to "see double", I was told – a favourite amusement of mine made possible by a tendency to squint; I must be careful in ball games and take my specs off for wrestling, rolling, turning head-over-heels and trying (always in vain) to stand on my head. I more or less observed these precautions, and only once did I break the precious lenses – a traumatic, guilt-laden experience, for I did it when playing a forbidden game, standing on the blade of a hoe and swinging on the handle. Even as the broken glass tinkled to the ground I knew that replacement would involve that scarce commodity, money, and that my own heedlessness was the cause. That was a bitter experience; when I recovered from a transport of guilt I found myself wickedly hoping that I might get out of "lessons" till I had specs again, but (quite rightly) I didn't.

Now turn from grief to ecstasy. For the very first time we are to be allowed a visit, with my mother, to the Flower Show. This is a village event of major importance, organised jointly by our village and the daughter parish across the fields, no doubt with a good deal of bickering behind the scenes, but always, it seems, attended by success on the actual day. This year it is the turn of our own village to host it, and my father, lifelong shunner of crowds and dreader of infection, has been persuaded that "the girls" would most likely survive, and even enjoy, going to the Show. Our inner excitement knows no bounds, though we have to keep it decently concealed till we are outside our white gate, dressed for the occasion in our Sunday best, Panama hats and all, and with a whole sixpence each to spend. What do we expect? No doubt my mother has told us of crowds, vast by village standards, of a tent full of flowers, fruit and vegetables, of bowling for a pig and of coconut shies. But nothing could prepare me for the heady rapture which I remember ever after as the Flower Show Feeling. It is a blend of excitement with scent, sight, and sound, concentrated inside the marquee which houses the lovingly tended exhibits from cottage and farmhouse gardens and kitchens. The smells of taut canvas, warm in the sun, and grass crushed underfoot, mingle with the fragrance of sweet peas, roses and stocks; faint good earthy scents arise from the scrubbed carrots and tight-skinned onions, the ruler-straight runner beans and fat red squatting tomatoes. Still more exciting are the aromas from the fruit section, where great black currants, long hidden under old net curtains on bushes, lie like miniature bunches of grapes alongside groups of rosy apples or golden greengages. Then on to the trestle table of home made cakes, each with a slice carefully cut out by the judges, flanked by bottled fruit and home made wines. It is a feast for the eye too, for not only are specimen prize flowers displayed in a perfection we have never seen before, but there is a class for "Best Mixed Bunch of Flowers in a Vase" – great masses of delphiniums, tiger lilies, roses, whatever can be brought on or held back for the Show. There is the children's special class "Best Bunch of Wild Flowers", where all our summer favourites meet – meadowsweet and honeysuckle, knapweed and fragile scarlet poppy, and yes! our best beloved meadow cranesbill. For the ear, there is the buzz and hum of two villages in holiday mood, circling round again and again inside the marquee, with a few preliminary discords from the local brass band penetrating festally now and then. Women and girls are fresh in their best cotton dresses, but the men and boys are soon red-faced and perspiring with the warmth of their good solid Sunday suits. They compare, admire, criticize; proud winners return again and again to see the coveted cards indicating "First Prize", or second, or third, next to their exhibit. Old Shep has carried off the prize for the best marrow as usual – how does he manage to bring them on so early? Charlie Bates, a comparative newcomer, has won the "Best Collection of Vegetables" class over the head of Bill Williams, the undisputed champion of eight years' standing. That will cost Charlie a few pints in the pub tonight. And can we really agree that Mrs Dolman's rich fruit cake is the finest – crunchy on top, moist fruit evenly distributed within, and baked to perfection, or have the judges been swayed by its display on a snowy white linen doily edged with hand-crocheted lace? Mrs Ball's cake, someone is sure to say, is a better one, only " 'er en't got none o' they fancy trimmings underneath'n to show 'n off like". There will be war in the Women's Institute later......

And when, surfeited at last with the atmosphere inside the marquee, we are persuaded outside into the fresh air, there are further thrills. Cups of tea are available, but that we can have at home – no wasting the precious sixpence on anything so common. Biliously yellow lemonade; pink, almost puce raspberryade; orangeade of a strange and violent hue – these we eye longingly, but they are forbidden, though other children are indulging in them with no apparent ill effects But an ice cream cornet at threepence – dare we, may we? We may and we do – in fact I have two, thus exhausting my sixpence, while Phil and Susie spend their other threepence on an unsuccessful attempt each at the coconut shy. We watch the bowling for the pig, a man's sport in the main – note their fierce concentration, for this prize is really worth having.

Knock, knock, thump, thump, over go the skittles, while the little pig, donated annually by a generous farmer who is on the Show Committee, trots disconsolately round the temporary pen in which he is on view, unaware that his home for the next few months is being determined. How nice it would be, I think dreamily, to have just one try – suppose that by a fluke I knocked down all the skittles, and amazed the whole village! "Well, did you ever now! Proper little skittler, bain't she! There then, my dear, you take 'e home – feed 'e all on scraps you may, see if 'ee can't". I would tuck him under my arm and carry him off and love him, and he would love me – my father would applaud my prowess, and we would build a little sty at the bottom of the garden and tend the little pig, oh so well......
From this improbable dream (anyone less likely than my father to welcome a pig at the bottom of the garden it would be hard to imagine) I am recalled to reality by my mother's voice saying it is time to go home. We plead for, and are allowed, one more walk round the marquee, now cooler and less crowded. Exhibitors are beginning to remove their treasures and to take their prize cards to the Committee table to claim their modest winnings. The trodden grass is turning brown, and there are sweet-papers and the ends of ice-cream cornets (fancy wasting them!), about which my mother will certainly have something to say to the children in school on Monday morning. Leaving, we debate taking my father an ice-cream – would he enjoy it? If we keep it lightly covered with a clean paper bag will he consider it sufficiently germ-free to consume? Even if he doesn't, surely he will be pleased at the thought? Somehow we scrape up the necessary threepence, and hurry home (pigless) before the ice-cream melts. Triumph – he both eats and enjoys it! That seems a fitting end to an afternoon of bliss; even in his self-chosen withdrawal, my father has had a share in the Flower Show Feeling.

As we grew older we were able to go occasionally to more sophisticated Shows a little further afield, complete with agricultural classes, riding and jumping, and so experienced the Feeling again. I have tasted it at Chelsea and Shrewsbury, and (blessed faculty of memory!) I can re-create it almost at will. But first is best, especially when treats are rare and senses are young and keen; for me, that very first Village Flower Show has never been bettered.

Lastly I must be allowed to stray a little beyond our earliest childhood in order to honour the second Vicarage family. When the shock waves caused by the retirement of the Old Vicar had passed, and the village took stock of the new arrivals, it did not take long to learn that we had been blessed with the advent of kindness and generosity personified. A few changes in the accepted order of things were accepted after a normal period of grumbling and head-shaking. My mother became organist, and a surpliced choir, which Phil, Susie and I joined with delirious joy, took shape. (Needless to say my mother took the making of some twenty surplices, plus black skirts and caps for the girls, nonchalantly in her stride). The School Treat was superseded by two Christmas parties, for under-8's and over-8's respectively, run and financed by "the Vicarage". It became our pleasure to help the Vicar's wife, surely one of the sweetest people who ever walked God's earth, and her daughters only a little older than ourselves, with the preparations, and to join in the fun. Over the buttering of buns, the filling of sandwiches and the replenishing of vast teapots and jugs of orangeade we thus met near-contemporaries with horizons far wider than our own. They brought a breath of fresh air into our lives, and gently, unwittingly, drew us a little out of our cocooned isolation towards maturity. We loved them not only for that, nor for the constant support which "the Vicarage" again

became, but for themselves; they shone like a good deed in a naughty world.

And the world was soon to become far, far naughtier than we had ever dreamed it could. Armistice Day had seemed the commemoration of something too frightful ever to recur, and the mounting world tensions of the 1930's were matters for grave discussion by the Grown-Ups above our heads, impinging little, and then with unreality, on our hill-cradled village and its sleepy ways, and still less on the three of us, absorbed in the business of childhood and growth. The awakening, when it came, was a rude one indeed. But the tale of the outbreak of war – of evacuees and rationing, of alternating precautions and defiance, of rabbit for dinner twice a week – does not belong to the carefree days of my childhood and so has no place here. I will only say that World War II left the village materially undamaged but took its toll from among the young men who went forth bravely and carelessly, never to return. More subtle was the effect on the soul of the village, for nothing was ever the same again. The war and its aftermath, as in many places, triggered off a process of village disintegration and decay. I am glad that I did not witness it, for we left the area soon after the end of the war, and for a long period of time I had no wish to re-visit it. Now, as I have said earlier, the village has taken a new lease of a different kind of life; it is for today's residents, in the intervals of commuting to Swindon or Chippenham or even further afield, to join the few remaining whose roots are in the old days, and to make of the village a place to live, not just to lodge in. But they will be hard put to it to re-create the pleasure and excitement in village events which was so intense and heady for us, and I fear that their cats will never have the measles.

Early Writings

As I draw near to the close of these journeyings back into my childhood, I am aware of viewing it, not exactly through rose-coloured spectacles, but through a succession of lenses, each of which has magnified some aspect perhaps even to the point of distortion. Or, to take another metaphor, I have pulled threads out here and there from the complex fabric of our lives and put them under a microscope, making each in turn appear of supreme importance, yet hoping to keep it in relation to the total pattern. I turn now to the last of these single strands, a smudgy, inky-coloured one with an unexpected gleam of brightness twisted into it here and there – the strand of writing.

To produce acceptable "handwriting", you will remember, was to me a process laborious to the point of despair and impossibility. Both impatience and myopia no doubt played their part in this; and I was never as naturally neat-fingered as Phil, though I liked, and still like, using my hands. I could however write after a fashion at quite an early age, as we all did. I have memories of Boxing Day sessions when, breathing heavily, we produced short stereotyped "thank you" letters to our relations at a distance. This was a task as burdensome as the handwriting "copies" we had to do in our exercise books, with double red and blue lines to regulate the sizes of different letters of the alphabet. But I suppose it opened up the possibilities of writing as a tool to be used for one's own ends. And of course children are great imitators. Surrounded as we were by books, it was natural, inevitable that we should turn to writing them ourselves.

It was an activity which absorbed and excited us, acceptable to the Grown-Ups, and not subject to the laws of perfection which governed "handwriting". The spoken word was already a rich plaything, notably in the context of our Dollands; the written word became another.

How I wish now that more of our early literary attempts had been preserved! As it is, I have to rely mainly on my fallible memory. It yields up first a poem – of sorts – written in pencil, in large sprawling letters, entitled "Spring".

The lake doth glitter
The thrush doth twitter
But on the ground
All in a mound
Is a big froggg hare.

Now all is dull
everything white
nice and cold
it is winter

lovley Spring
Lovley buds
Lovley evrything.

I remember that I did not take this effusion too seriously, nor did anyone else. I thought (how misguidedly!) that the first two lines were "proper poetry", but I knew very well that I had then got tired of it and finished it off anyhow. And why was my hare "froggg"? I think I pictured him rather limp and flabby after the winter, lying in a state of collapse which somehow suggested a frog. I had meant to write "froggy", but my treacherous pencil went on forming g's of its own volition, which put an effective end to the poem and made it a family joke for some time.

Then there was "Mrs. Hop", which unlike most of my early works was dated; I was about six when I produced this –

Mrs. Hop, Went hop hop hop,
In a race she was always the winner
One day she ate such a big diner
She went Pop!

The family quite liked Mrs Hop.

But the next effort which I can recall was more ambitious. My father regularly received Jonathan Cape's literary journal "Now And Then", in which there was an occasional children's competition. Phil and I both entered for one, the assignment being to write the story of how one of the characters from a children's book published by Cape had come to tea. Hugh Lofting's "Dr. Dolittle" books were among our favourites, and I chose, or was guided to choose, a visit by Gub-Gub the pig. I remember that he disliked the food I offered and asked for parsnips, but otherwise the story line is weak. To our surprise it was awarded a prize (a book or books of my own choice), and childlike, I rejoiced greatly, with little thought, I fear, for Phil's stoically unspoken disappointment. The typed letter which I received (what glory! a typed letter!) asked me to tell Phil that the judge had liked her story very much and that it might have won a prize too if we hadn't been in the same age group; this was a piece of reasoning with which, at the age of six, I was quite unable to cope.

Over the next few years, it seems to me, there was usually some literary work on hand. I dreamed of achieving "a proper published book", identifying myself in this (and other) respects with Jo in "Little Women". I was reputed to share some of her worse characteristics – untidiness, tactlessness and clumsiness – but her "scribbling" was a respectable activity for me to emulate. I started book after book with great panache, but few survived beyond halfway through the first chapter. This was, alas, typical of many of my pursuits; my oddments box told a sad story of enthusiastic beginnings – writing, embroidery, knitting, next year's family Christmas presents – relegated thither at an early stage in their abortive careers. I remember feeling really oppressed at one time by the number of my unfinished projects, and even worrying over my own moral weakness in not getting on with them. Phil was so much more persevering, and Susie seemed better at gauging her own abilities and did not start what she couldn't complete. Both of them wrote too, sometimes secretively – "No, you're not to see it till it's finished" – and sometimes with open pride. Occasionally we collaborated; some of the transient compositions used in our play – the marbles songs, for instance – I have already recorded. These built up spontaneously, one of us bursting out with a line and another completing the couplet with more rhyme than reason. I don't think they were ever written down. "Moley and Coley" was another of this kind; Susie was the envied possessor of two small brown moles on one arm, which we personified under these names. We invented a game of dancing our hands on a flat surface, while chanting –

"Moley and Coley danced upon the shore
Free from any care.
Their mother said 'You must go to bed,
For you're in danger there.' "

At "there" all the hands scampered off into hiding with as much confusion as possible, to come out for a repeat performance till we were tired of the game, which sounds a feeble one now but was hugely enjoyable at the time. On the whole, though, we ran more to prose than to verse. Phil's major work extended over a long period, but she was shy of exposing it even to our limited public; consequently I have only an impression that it had a farm or country theme, that it was "a real book with chapters", and that it contained a good many lyrical descriptions of "nature" with crayon illustrations by the author. A lovingly coloured sunrise (or sunset?) I do recall, captioned "Tinging the clouds… with purple and gold", which I thought supremely beautiful. I must have been allowed an occasional peep when Phil was feeling expansive, unless (horrid thought!) I broke our code by looking in her desk when she and Susie had Gone For The Milk one day.

Susie, for once, gloried openly in the work of hers which I remember best. She was badly affected by those rip-roaring thunderstorms of our childhood, and my mother used to tell her to "cheer up, it's only the giants up in the sky throwing bricks about". Nobody was meant to believe this, but it was good for a laugh, and mitigated the thunder to some extent. Susie turned it into a very spirited story which she wrote out neatly in print, like a proper story – remember that we had learned to write an almost copperplate longhand, so that to print anything was quite a refinement, as well as a considerable effort. A whole family of giants lived up in the sky, and a big box of wooden bricks appeared as a plaything for the baby giants; the lightning was their flashing teeth when they smiled with pleasure, the thunder followed when they tiped (sic) the bricks out of the box, and the rain was their tears when they had to put the bricks away and go to bed. Pretty good for Susie, we all thought. Another story of hers revolved round the King and Queen of the Butterflies, but all I can dredge up of this is that at some point the Queen exclaimed to the King "Oh you beautiful creature". Susie's really deathless effort, however, was a short poem –

Now summer is crawling around us,
The flowers look happy and gay
We take our dolls out in the garden,
And dance with them in May.

We all appreciated this, and used to sing it to the tune of one of the Infant Class songs which we had picked up. In spite of its wicked racialist tendencies I must insert it as a period piece –

I have a black dolly called Topsy
Who doesn't like sleeping alone,
For Topsy's afraid of the shadows,
Though in darkness I'm sure there are none.
But Topsy is only a dolly
And doesn't know better, you see.
So I just tuck her under my pillow,
For I know she likes sleeping with me.

And when the sun shines in the morning
I sing till I think she's awake.
Then I take her right out in the garden
And give her a bath in the lake.
But Topsy gets blacker and blacker,
Though shiny as shiny can be.
Though I wash her and wash her and wash her,
She'll ne-ver be whi-ite like me.

(When I acquired a black doll made of "competition" I automatically called her Topsy, and having no lake in which to bath her I once buttered her all over to make her "shiny as shiny can be").

I did compose quite a creditable "poem" in ballad style and even made up a simple tune for it –

In Maylia lives a pretty girl,
Blow the bugle loud!
Her hair is bright with many a curl,
Blow the bugle loud!

Her eyes are blue as summer skies,
Blow the bugle loud!
Her golden hair about her flies
Blow the bugle loud!

Her name's as fair as she herself,
Blow the bugle loud!
Her name is Vera Hazelelf,
Blow the bugle loud!

Vera's my love and e'er shall be,
Blow the bugle loud!
I love her and she loves me,
Blow the bugle loud!

This went down very well even with the Grown-Ups.

But on the whole, as I have said, we preferred prose; and it was pretty derivative prose at that, clearly reflecting whatever we were reading at the time, though we would have hotly denied any charges of plagiarism. We had a phase of books, some our own and some from the County Library so conveniently next door in school, about pioneers in the colonies. How I would now love to re-read "A Little Rhodesian", "Gwenda's Friend from Home", "Dingo Boys", "Kenya Kiddies", and others of that ilk, whose several authors I have, alas, forgotten. They inspired me to start on my own "Settlers in Africa", which died an early death after an unconvincing adventure with a lion. I also embarked on a collection of short stories; again I am sure they were strongly derivative, though I can't recall the source. "Violet's Race" is a fair sample. Violet runs a race for the honour of her school, and of course wins it, in spite of losing both shoes en route. As she staggers away from the tape her teacher approaches her. "Violet" she said softly "you have run well. May you always do everything as well". Posterity, I feel, has not lost much by my ceasing to produce this genre.

At about the same time, judging by the writing (for these fragments I do still possess) came "The House of Higgins", three whole chapters of it, in pencil, with rather angular drawings featuring Higgins, his friend Sam Green, his wife Eliza, their six children and Higgins' Aunt Priscilla – all apparently wooden-limbed, for I never could manage arms and legs. We must, I think, have recently encountered Cockney speech in some book or other, for "The House of Higgins" is really just a vehicle for presenting my own peculiar version of Cockney, and the action is quite secondary. The first chapter describes Bill H. and his friend trying to catch escaped chickens, but they do little but address each other – " 'Elp me,

'Iggins – I only got one on 'em and 'e's loose again now". Chapter II, "Mrs Higgins on Strike", has dramatic possibilities, but gets no further than some acrimonious exchanges on the cooking of breakfast, with plentiful dropping and adding of h's. In Chapter III Higgins' children, ranging from Elsie, aged fourteen, to Jenny, aged four, are briefly described "Twelve year old Jane followed. She despised her sisters and had a large head" well, that she had to have, as I had already drawn her, accidentally, with a rather hydrocephalic appearance. Tom, the only boy, was "mad about ball games" and intended to become a champion footballer, although "the others tried to make him understand that he couldn't make his living by being a footballer". (Evidently Tom was born too soon). But it was a laboured work, and petered out early in Chapter IV; a pity, for the sudden visit of Higgins' Aunt Priscilla (in my books visitors tended to invite themselves, leaving no chance of a refusal) with "'Loiza" in bed with 'flu, had possibilities, could I have seen them through my current haze of h's.

In a later phase during which we devoured Brownie and Girl Guide stories, I started my own, entitled "The Girls of Edmouth". The theme was a well-worn one – newcomer to village starts Guide Company and reforms wild village girls – and I got several chapters into this, enjoying the young author's privilege of a blissful disregard for probability. We had a little book of "Christian Names And Their Meanings" on the shelf, and I ransacked it for names for the chief characters, scattering Yvonnes, Dorindas, Berengarias and Melissas over Edmouth in careless abandon. Melissa Eliot, the heroine, forms a Guide Company at the drop of a hat, selling the idea to the village girls as "uncommonly jolly" – no red tape, a large barn offered as a meeting place, no jealousy caused by an arbitrary choice of Patrol Leaders at the first meeting. All rather a far cry from the realities of village life!

I had at this stage, as well as a burning enthusiasm for Guides, a passion for toddlers, so one of my village girls had to bring her baby brother to the meetings, which created some would-be humorous diversions. There is an interlude in which Melissa and Yvonne fish for treasure in the village pond, catching nothing but an old boot filled with mud; this has no relation to the main theme, but I never allowed trifles like that to worry me. A lieutenant (Dorinda) offers herself conveniently for service ("I think Guiding is such a wonderful Movement. And now that it has come to Edmouth I want to share in it"), but once more we end abruptly, in mid-sentence this time, while Melissa is explaining to Dorinda that Guides do "anything jolly and at the same time useful". "Jolly" was a great word in my childhood. "The Girls of Edmouth" was followed by "The Company Good Turn", again combining Guides and toddlers. Captain and older Guides volunteered to camp (in a Hut) for a week, looking after three small children, also accommodated in the Hut, to enable their hard-pressed mothers to have a holiday. This work only got to the beginning of Chapter II – arrival of the first toddler "with his toothbrush wrapped in greaseproof paper" before my interest waned, or my powers of invention gave out.

I produced a fair amount of "The Pet Lamb", a monotonous story of one Annie Brown, whose life revolved around a hand-reared lamb; with only feeble opposition from her parents, Annie kept the lamb in her bedroom and took it everywhere she went, including shopping in town and camping with the Guides. (Guides again). The inevitable thunderstorm figures once more, and there is a period of snowy weather in which the luckless lamb is taken out for walks wearing a warm suit knitted by Annie, complete with little woolly boots. After a rather splendidly defiant opening "From the time that they were born to now Annie Brown had loved the two little lambs.

Yes, and she intended to go on loving them" – the work becomes so dull that I shall quote it no further; it peters out in the middle of the Guide Camp, which is apparently a totally disorganised affair.

But I did finish one book, and that was a record for the three of us – one "proper book with chapters", and I have it still. "Joan and the Twins" was perhaps the least derivative of all my literary works, for it was a "family" story which revolved round some of the favourite characters from my Dolland. "Miss Alison and her three adopted children lived in a comfortable old farmhouse…" it began (you will remember that men were largely excluded from my Dolland, so Miss Alison was unencumbered by a husband, but adoption ensured respectability). And it lasted for fourteen chapters (short ones!) carefully printed in ink on narrow-lined pages, each with a suitable crayoned illustration. I used one side of the paper only, as I had gathered from Jo's efforts in "Little Women" that this was correct when preparing one's work for publication. Miss A. had apparently unlimited means, and was thus able to give her adopted family, as a matter of course, all the treats which we enjoyed as rarities – going to the seaside or the Zoo, for instance – as well as others only dreamed of, such as staying with a rather cross Aunt Jane (we would have loved that, we thought, however cross she had been), a trip on a houseboat, the purchase of a dog, and that of two new horses, Velvet and Night. They were "pitch black and as shiny as if they had been polished. Of course, it was really only that they had had plenty of butter in their oats". There were thinly disguised accounts of some of our own everyday events too – those dramatic thunderstorms again, the building of a "house" in the garden with "branchy sticks and hay". There was some attempt at characterization – one of the twins, Mabel, was bustling, confident and full of ideas, while Agnes was shyer, more sensitive, and given to headaches. Little Joan was characterized mainly by her imperfect speech. There were touches of humour. The houseboat trip was a disaster, as it rained most of the week; this I think was inevitable, as my imagination refused to supply suitable events apart from the sighting of an otter. There were some very laboured endings to chapters, governed apparently by my desire to get to the end of the page. And there was the usual fine disregard for probability when the family, out for a walk "by the side of Lake Sparkle, a large pond about fifty yards away" encountered a beggar girl and adopted her on the spot, with no formalities and no subsequent problems. The book ended three chapters later with the celebration of Gwen's birthday. "Gwen was very happy, for it was her tenth birthday and her birthday had never been celebrated before". There were presents from everyone. "At teatime of course Gwen said she would cut all the slices of cake, and of course she didn't, as it's harder than it looks to cut cake, and of course the cake was pronounced delicious, which it was...... They had a lovely day, and here we leave them" – a conclusion which, after much head-scratching and pen-chewing, (you can chew a wooden pen-holder!) I lifted shamelessly from "The Hunter Children", another great favourite now lost. Better authors than myself have, I believe, had similar problems. I really did yearn to send "Joan and the Twins" to a publisher. But my father paid me the compliment of reading it right though, taking it quite seriously, and then "advised" me against trying to get it published. As I couldn't have got hold of so much as a penny stamp without his knowledge, "advice" was pretty effective. He did manage not to deflate me, though, for he said that if I went on writing, I might later become "quite a good writer of children's stories".

He was wrong there – at least so far – for although I have tried children's stories I have never risen above the utterly banal, and there is quite enough of that already. He was probably right in his judgement that "Joan and the Twins" was no candidate for publication. It lacks the sophistication of "The Young Visiters", and the fact that it is much better spelt would probably have been a drawback. But it is an endearing work, with touches of originality ("The garden was divided into eight parts; the first for flowers, the second for vegetables" and so on through fungi, ferns, mosses, ponds, trees, " and the eighth, well, that was the rock garden"), and I am still proud to own it.

I continued to hanker after appearing in print, however, and the children's section of the "Farmer's Weekly" (bless its daffodil-yellow cover) seemed to offer the best chances. Susie and I entered for various story-writing competitions here. (I think Phil was by now too heavily committed to "lessons", or maybe she had broken some age barrier). Usually a few elements were supplied, such as "twins, a kitten, a snowstorm and some small coins," and one had to weave the story around them. I scored at least one small prize (a postal order for 2/6) as well as seeing Susie take a prize over my head, just as I had done over Phil's in the "Now And Then" competition some years before. I hope I had no hard feelings. And I appeared a couple of times in "The Guide", with a letter to the Patrol Leaders' page, and a lively account of a hike in the pouring rain; here I first encountered the infuriating power of editors to lop off half a sentence or omit one's most telling phrase. I have grown to expect it after scattered journalistic efforts in later life, but it still outrages my author's soul.

A brief excursion into literary criticism (I was nothing if not versatile) also returns to mind, although why it has stuck verbatim with me, I have no idea. "Today" I wrote, "I read

Poe's poem 'The Raven' for the first time. A grand poem. To take one example 'Quoth the Raven, Nevermore.' Is not that a grand line?" And here, as usual, I ground to a halt. I have a suspicion that I had been dipping into Phil's copy of "The Conversations of Dr. Johnson", for my final sentence has a slightly Johnsonian ring; actually there were odd bits in the "Conversations" which I could understand at least better than I could "The Raven".

I must have gone on scribbling, by fits and starts, till well into my teens, when The Exam began to dominate my life to the exclusion of all else for a time. The last work which I will inflict on the reader is a joint one, mainly in the form of parodied Nursery Rhymes. For some reason – don't ask me why or how – the three of us invented a character named Banktuviski, and started to compile –

THE BANKTUVISKI Book (sic)

being

The Authentic history of the daring exploits of

Kospef Boskov Banktuviski,

an extremely wicked Russian Communist, dark and sinister. He wears a black cloak, out of which he slips when arrested, and carries pistols which he does not scruple to use. Has been in prison, but always escapes. Also of

Petrov Leapovitch Banktuviski,

fairly wicked, his brother, and used as a tool by the elder Banktuviski.

The book starts with a really brilliant effort from Susie –

The eel of Inverness

(which was something like the Loch Ness Monster. One brother had been to sea and found the other on a ship when he returned).

Kosp.   Brother, I wish that we could catch the eel so lithe and frisky.

For that would be a fitting deed for the Brothers Banktuviski.

Petr.　But brother, I have caught the little eel of Inverness.

Kosp.　But brother, you have turned the deck into a nasty mess.

Petr.　Brother, I couldn't help it, and I did lure him out
　　　By holding o'er the bulwarks a large and juicy trout.

Kosp.　Brother, you should have waited till I could come again.

Petr.　Brother, the night was very dark, it teemed and poured with rain.
　　　Brother, I thought that you would never come again to me.
　　　Brother, I thought that you were lying at the bottom of the sea.
　　　At any rate, my brother, I piped the eel aboard.

Kosp.　But brother, look around you, and see what he has gnawed.

Petr.　Brother, I have got him safely in the hold
　　　And brother, I forgot to say, the night was very cold
　　　And I gave the eel of Inverness a bed of nice warm hay.

Kosp.　Brother, you should have waited till I could say you nay.

Petr.　Brother, I did give him a beefsteak for to eat,
　　　For I thought it couldn't hurt him to be breakfasting on meat.

Kosp.　Brother you should have waited, but still, alive we've got him.

Petr.　Brother, I forgot to say, he bit me, so I shot him.

After this episode the brothers turned to really dark deeds, and the parodies began. We all contributed, singly or in collaboration, though I seem to remember that Phil did so with the air of an elder statesman kindly joining in childish things.

Rest awhile, Kospef, in prison cell,
Judges and jury your fate soon will tell.
Here comes the judge, black cap and all.
Come along, Kospef, the axe soon will fall!
(but he got away in time, as usual).

Then there was –

Kospef had a little gun, its barrel bright as day.
And everywhere that Kospef went, it went too all the way.
He took it into jail, although his pockets they did feel.
It made the other prisoners quake to see that glint of steel!

And even –

Banktuviski, lithe and frisky, how does your pistol go?
With a click and a clang, and a spark and a bang,
And bullet-holes all in a row, row, row!

I confess that I am now a little puzzled, not to say shocked, by the degree of cheerful bloodthirstiness revealed in the Banktuviski poems; it is hardly consistent with the image one would like to have of one's childhood self. And yet... in creep hazy recollections of an episode of whipping our dolls with nettles, to the strong disapproval of the Grown-Ups. There was the Junior Soldiers game which enthralled Susie and me for some time; we dressed a number of our dolls in military uniforms made from old sheets, and put them gleefully through a course of severe Army discipline at a quite tender age (I refer here to the assumed age of the dolls, for training as a Junior Soldier could begin from the age of ten months). And, again with Susie as partner, I once conducted a doll's hanging. The occasion was our discovery of extensive moth holes in some of our stock of dolls' clothes; we were so furious that we dressed up a soft doll (probably the luckless Alec who had been so uncooperative in the matter of being ground to powder in the wheel of the sewing machine) to look as moth-like as possible, and then hanged the moth in effigy – a phrase which had caught our fancy. Perhaps, then, I must face the facts and acknowledge that we had our share of bloodthirstiness, or aggression – call it what you will – and that it had to find a channel of expression from time to time.

Anyway, I am glad that we committed Kospef and Petrov to paper; I only wish that I could trace their origin, but that is completely lost. They stand, pistols in hand, all ready to slip out of those sinister black cloaks into the obscurity from which they came, an unexplained last fling of our childish imaginations. Like the other works which I have quoted, perhaps at too great length, they leave behind them a sense of fun, and of the joy of even an unfinished creation. And if, dear reader, (as they used to say) *you* are not a creature of my imagination, rejoice with me that I have at last achieved my ambition – a proper published book.

Somewhere below a wooded hill,
Beyond the reach of place and time,
My childhood village drowses still –
The cock still crows, the church bells chime.

The faithful seasons pass and bring
Their timeless tasks in plot and field.
Bleak Winter sires ecstatic Spring,
Rich Summer dies in Autumn's yield.

Memory alone fresh life can give
To scenes of childhood's eager joys.
Kind Memory bids the old folks live,
Keeps young the village girls and boys.

Daily the bell insistent calls –
From farm and cottage, come to school!
And chanting drones through grey stone walls
Where "Governess" holds her kindly rule.

The country sounds my childhood knew
Clutch at my heart across the years.
A milk churn's clang, a shrill cuckoo,
Chattering starlings, rend to tears.

Remember how our hearts, carefree,
Made festival of each new day?
Hailing its dawn with noisy glee,
Cramming its hours with busy play –

Feeding each sense with keen delight,
Making our own the wealth around –
The sunwarmed turf, the swallow's flight,
The smell of hay, the anvil's sound.

These were the roots from which we sprang,
These were our daily drink and meat.
We were the song the skylark sang,
We were the chalk beneath our feet.

We are the beech tree's soaring bole,
We are the cranesbill's mystic blue,
We have their substance in our soul –
Roots immemorial, earthy, true –

Ourselves the fabric that they wove
Across the threads of daily life,
Shot through with all our parents' love,
Our childish harmony and strife.

Now, fifty mellowing years away,
Dipping the sources whence I came,
I know my truest self today
Still inescapably the same.

I thank my God that I may keep
My inner continuity.
The child I was is but asleep –
That questing child who still is me.

And somewhere, free of time and place,
Winds on the dear familiar lane
Where our small selves forever pace,
Going to fetch the milk again.

About the Author

Alison Hartfield spent her childhood in an isolated village in North Wiltshire, and subsequently trained as a teacher of young children at Salisbury. She has taught in both Infant and Nursery Schools, and has also spent nearly twenty years as a lecturer in the field of teacher training. She has published an anthology of poems for young children, and occasional contributions to educational journals.

Alison Hartfield is now retired, rejoicing that this has given her the opportunity to return to life in the country.

About the Illustrator

Judith Wall trained as an artist and teacher at The Bath Academy of Art, Corsham. Her work, mostly quite large 'abstract' landscape paintings, has been exhibited in Bath and Bristol.

Having taught Art for several years in Secondary Schools, she then took some time out to bring up two children. Later she returned, this time teaching in a Further Education College, which involved managing the Art Department. She did this for several years before retiring.